OPEN YOUR MIND
TO
PROSPERITY

OTHER BOOKS BY THE AUTHOR:

THE DYNAMIC LAWS OF PROSPERITY
THE DYNAMIC LAWS OF HEALING
THE PROSPERITY SECRET OF THE AGES
THE HEALING SECRET OF THE AGES
PRAY AND GROW RICH
THE PROSPERING POWER OF LOVE
THE SECRET OF UNLIMITED PROSPERITY
OPEN YOUR MIND TO RECEIVE
DARE TO PROSPER!
THE PROSPERING POWER OF PRAYER

****

"The Millionaires of the Bible" Series:

THE MILLIONAIRES OF GENESIS,
Their Prosperity Secrets for You

THE MILLIONAIRE MOSES,
His Prosperity Secrets for You

THE MILLIONAIRE JOSHUA,
His Prosperity Secrets for You

THE MILLIONAIRE FROM NAZARETH,
His Prosperity Secrets for You

OPEN YOUR MIND TO PROSPERITY

Catherine Ponder

Published by
DeVORSS & COMPANY
P.O. Box 550, Marina del Rey, CA 90294

ISBN: 0-87516-531-1
Library of Congress Catalog Card Number: 70-155720

Printed in the United States of America

CONTENTS

PART I

BASIC METHODS FOR
DEMONSTRATING PROSPERITY

Why you must open your mind to prosperity. How to open your
mind to prosperity. Reports of those who have prospered. Prosperity
came to all those who helped with the author's first book. A report from
the typesetter of this book. The true definition of prosperity. There are
millionaires in the Bible! The Bible is a prosperity textbook. Prosperity
is necessary for your growth. True prosperity has a spiritual basis. This
attitude is practical.

How others have been helped by this secret text. How the prospering power of the Christ worked for the author. The prospering power of the Lord's Prayer. Casual affirmations work, too. How casual words prospered a janitor.

Tithing, a millionaire's formula. You can tithe your way out of indebtedness. When you cannot afford to tithe. Tithing your time isn't enough. Withholding the tithe brings lack. Where you give is important. Tithing heals. Where you give your money is where you give your faith. Gross or net? What the author learned from withholding a tithe. When something is taken from you. Tithing brings good in all phases of your life. A special note from the author.

PART II

OTHER WAYS TO DEMONSTRATE PROSPERITY

The easy way to unfold your good. The author's childhood sense of a divine plan. How a housewife manifested the divine plan for her life. How to clear the wrong people out of your life. The divine plan often brings changes. How to free yourself from an old cycle. How to pray successfully for yourself and others. When your good is delayed.

True education wells up from within. How the wisdom concept prospers. Realtor becomes millionaire through the wisdom concept. How dentist prospers through wisdom concept. Dress designer goes from poverty to affluence. How a man prospered from using scrap tin. How the wisdom concept heals and prospers an attorney. Affirmations release wisdom. Job transfer comes through the wisdom concept. Divine wisdom works in otherwise uncontrollable situations. Solomon's costly mistake. The wisdom concept is easy to use.

Love concept develops a harmonious attitude. How the love concept helps neighbors. How the love concept heals. The freeing power of love. Love and wisdom united.

The word *loss* means destruction. Decree of fulfillment blots out loss. How to heal the unhappiness of the past. A period of gain, not loss. Businessman gets better job. Former prisoner restored to good life. The ancient secret of restoration. How divine restoration improved their lives. Decree of restoration brings new love. How to call on divine restoration. Restoration comes under divine timing.

Prosperous thinking may bring changes.

Introduction....

IT'S TIME TO PROSPER!

A Special Message from the Author

Decked out in a fashionable pants suit, an attractive Southern California businesswoman once said to the author:

"When I first began to use the power of prosperous thinking, I prospered so much that it startled me. Just divorced, with only a few months' income on hand, I decided to take a chance and go into business on a shoestring. I expected to make four to five thousand dollars the first year. Instead, through the use of your formula, I made almost five thousand dollars the first few months. I am now on the way to a $50,000-per-year income, and my greatest problem has been in trying not to feel guilty about being so prosperous."

A mother and daughter learned of this formula and used it when both were out of work. The daughter then won an audition to be in a production of "The Music Man." On the same day that she won the audition, her mother was given a job in the entertainment field, too. "A bonus for daring to think prosperously," commmented the mother. Later, the daughter appeared on national television. She has continued in show business.

Another report was this: "Our house was about to be repossessed. Our finances were in a deplorable state. Then I began applying your prosperity formula. Wonderful things began happening. We received a check in the mail for ten thousand dollars. It was an inheritance from a relative, who had passed on a few months earlier. Ordinarily these business details take months to settle. We knew this relative had left us something, but we never dreamed it would be so much."

Still another declared: "If it weren't for the power of prosperous thinking, I would be in jail with unpaid debts. Instead I am now married to a wonderful, talented, loving man. I am prospering beyond my former wildest beliefs, and I am now writing articles and books, all of which are being published."

She explained: "A year ago 'the law' was after me for unpaid debts, I was just out of the hospital after an operation, I had gotten fired from my job, and I was lonely with no one to love. At that time I was depressed, broke, and ill.

"Then I learned your prosperity philosophy and began using it. In short order, I got a monthly series of articles in three magazines. I again found the man I loved. We had dated briefly several years before, then drifted apart. Suddenly everything fell into place. Now, a few months later, I find myself the author of two books and many articles, married to the man I love, and wonderfully prosperous."

Incredible?

Impossible?

Not at all. These are simply the results of prosperous thinking.

HOW THIS PROSPERITY FORMULA WAS BORN

This book contains a simple formula for invoking "the power of prosperous thinking"—a formula that was twenty years in the making.

The author began searching for such a formula several decades ago when she was a secretary, widowed, with a child to support—alone.

As she searched the bookshelves, studied the lives of famous people, sought out the success formulas mystically given in the Bible, and took up the study of the "New Thought" philosophy, she began to ferret out prosperity's formulas bit by bit. Then she pursued the power of prosperous thinking through two careers: first as a secretary, then as a non-denominational minister.

When the worst recession since World War II hit the United States in 1958, the formulas for prosperity began to unfold to her in an orderly sequence as she taught prosperity classes in her first ministry in Birmingham, Alabama.

From the research developed for those classes, and as a result of the exciting results received by those in attendance, she began writing about prosperity: first, in a non-denominational publication for business people; then, through her first book, *The Dynamic Laws of Prosperity*. Now, decades later, that book continues to transform the lives of people on a worldwide basis, through its various translations.

THE AUTHOR'S PROGRESS

Her life, too, was transformed, as she finished her work in the "magic city" in the Deep South, and moved on. She originally went to Texas to conduct prosperity lectures for two weeks. Instead, she stayed twelve years, founded two churches, and wrote almost a dozen books. As a result of studying with her during that period, a number of her students became New Thought ministers, and were also instrumental in the founding of additional churches.

In 1970 her prosperity writings and lectures nationwide had proved so popular that a Unity editor, Charles Lelly, asked if she could develop a new prosperity book for the Unity Press. Since she had just spent ten years traveling from coast to coast giving her "gold dust lectures," *Open Your Mind to Prosperity* was the result.

Now, more than a decade later, as she updates this book, she is grateful to the officials of Unity School of Christianity for allowing her to have it reissued by her California publisher, through which it can continue to reach an ever-increasing readership.

As might be expected, the prosperity methods described in this book have led the author into a happier, more productive life. The work of her now-global ministry reaches into all fifty of the United States, and into as many foreign countries. She enjoys living and working in a beautiful resort area located in the metaphysical consciousness of Southern California. Although she is no longer able to honor the many lecture requests that pour in from all over the world, she looks forward to continuing a full work and writing schedule for many years to come. Accolades for a lifetime of such intensive work include an honorary doctorate, listings in *Who's Who* and the *Social Register*.

A READER'S PROGRESS REPORT

The reports of readers, who have been helped by this book, are too numerous to recount. The following letter is but one of the many reports received by the author over the years:

About two years ago, when working in a cosmetic sales area, I was encouraged by my beautiful sales director to read *Open Your Mind to Prosperity*.

That was the beginning of an exciting new life for me. On pure faith, I applied the principles set forth in that book, and demonstrations were inevitable. Within a few months my business prospered, I became a sales director myself, and met my husband-to-be.

Although I had previously lived on meager means in a small rented house, we now have a beautiful home in the exclusive Bel-Air area of Los Angeles. Johnny Carson, the Gabors, and many famous show business personalities have estates nearby.

Since I no longer have to work, I now devote most of my time to my first love, the spiritual path. I spend time helping others learn to apply the prosperity formulas I have learned. What a joy! I thank God every day for having led me to that book.

WHAT THIS PROSPERITY FORMULA CONTAINS

Why have some people literally gone from "rags to riches" through following the ideas given in these pages? Well, in this present book, the author is sharing with you her succinct formula for prosperity, which has evolved slowly over the years and which she gives in its completed form here for the first time.

Open Your Mind to Prosperity, originally written in 1971, is a sequel to *The Dynamic Laws of Prosperity*, which was first published in 1962. From the time the author conducted her first prosperity class in 1958, and from the time of the publication of her first prosperity article in 1959, the results have always been the same: an enthusiastic request for more material on the subject, and countless unsolicited reports of what, at times, seemed like miraculous results by those who used these prosperity methods.

There are many success courses and books available today, and they are all good. Anything that helps you to open
your mind to prosperity is worthwhile.

But *most of those courses and books cover only about one-fourth of
the formula given in this book.* They usually explain how to create your prosperity mentally first, as shown in Chapters 3, 4
and 5 herein.

But unless you learn how to clear away the psychological
blocks about prosperity, as discussed in Chapter 1; unless
you then learn how to cleanse your mind to make way for
prosperity, as explained in Chapter 2; and unless you follow
this up by giving your prosperity a spiritual basis, as shown
in Chapter 6—just creating your prosperity mentally first is
not enough.

The acts of creating your prosperity mentally first may
excite you into bringing about temporary results. Then you
sink down into frustration and despair again as these results
fade away, and you say to yourself, "It doesn't really work."

By learning the *entire* formula for prosperity as given in
this book, in both Part I and Part II, you will find that it becomes an automatic process which you can easily invoke
again and again, and you will enjoy doing so.

For instance, when your prosperity seems to slacken, you
will know that you must again consciously open your mind
to prosperity by reminding yourself often, "I AM THE RICH
CHILD OF A LOVING FATHER, SO I DARE TO PROSPER."

Then you will return to the cleansing laws of prosperity
and again form a vacuum, in both inner and outer ways.
You will begin anew to create your prosperity mentally
first, probably making a new list, getting fresh mental pictures and affirmations to work with daily. And you will happily use "ten, the magic number of increase" in your giving.

In due time you will probably go from ten percent to
larger giving, as allowed for tax purposes, and as provided

by the Mosaic law many centuries ago. This one prosperity technique alone made millionaires of many of the Bible's great people, as well as many of our modern millionaires.

You will also enjoy using the prosperity methods described in Part II, and find them helpful toward demonstrating results.

THE AUTHOR'S INVITATION

In the intervening years, since this book, *Open Your Mind to Prosperity* was written (1971) as a sequel to *The Dynamic Laws of Prosperity* (1962), the author has recently written yet another book: a "sequel to the sequel," entitled *Open Your Mind to Receive* (1983).[1] You will find these three books an appropriate trilogy on the fascinating subject of universal abundance.

As you use again and again the prosperity laws described in this present book, and in the others mentioned, you will find yourself agreeing with the author that "It's time to prosper!" And you will probably find yourself motivated to pass on this timely message to others.

As you do so, she invites you to write her of your happy results in increased peace, health and plenty.

> Catherine Ponder
> P.O. Drawer 1278
> Palm Desert, California 92261
> U.S.A.

---

1. *Open Your Mind to Receive* (Marina del Rey, CA: DeVorss & Co., 1983).

PART I

BASIC METHODS FOR DEMONSTRATING PROSPERITY

OPEN YOUR MIND TO PROSPERITY

— Chapter 1 —

I declared war on poverty when I was still in the first grade. We lived in a poverty-stricken area of the South, and most of the children in my school had neither adequate lunches nor enough clothes.

When my mother gave me lunch money, I just gave it away. Upon learning what I was doing, she began preparing my lunches. This made me very happy. It meant I could step up my war on poverty as I broke up sandwiches and passed them out to my classmates.

Mother never was able to stop me from giving away my lunches. But when I started giving away my clothes she objected strongly. Finally she said: "We cannot afford to clothe the entire neighborhood—though we almost have this winter, thanks to you. I'm going to buy you one more coat, and you'd better not give it away."

One cold winter day I arrived home from school, obedi-
ently wearing that winter coat, but barefooted. I had just
given away my shoes and socks! It was not until years later
that I learned how to wage war on poverty in such a way
that I did not have to give away my lunches, my shoes, or
my socks.

A Wall Street economist recently gave his formula for
a cure for poverty: "What is needed is not so much a war
on poverty as an understanding of the forces that generate
prosperity."

WHY YOU MUST OPEN YOUR MIND TO PROSPERITY

The forces that generate prosperity are mental and spiritual. In order to conduct a mental and spiritual war on
poverty, the first thing you must do is open your mind to
prosperity.

I came upon this great truth quite by accident. I was a
minister in Birmingham, Alabama, when the worst recession since World War II hit this country.

Birmingham is an industrial city. During that recession,
it was so hard hit economically that thousands of people
were out of work. There were breadlines; everyone was
talking depression, hard times, and lack; finally the government declared the city a disaster area, making federal aid
available.

It was during that trying period that the people in my
church asked me to teach a class that would point out the
mental and spiritual laws of prosperity.

I soon discovered something significant. Even though the
people in that class desperately needed to be prospered,
most of them had the old, erroneous idea that it was sinful
to be prosperous. *They felt guilty about even coming to a prosperity
class.*

Since that time I have discovered that there is nothing unusual in this attitude. Most people with financial problems have a psychological block about prosperity. They have been taught in the past that poverty is a Christian virtue, and that to be prosperous is somehow wicked. They have been taught that anyone who is prosperous is probably a crook and therefore subject to suspicion. In any event, he is a "sinner."

How in the world can poverty be a Christian virtue, when poverty causes most of the world's problems?

Communism has a poverty basis. An economist has said that the main difference between democracy and communism might be described in one word: "plenty" or "prosperity." Prosperous people do not want or need communism.

Not only are both war and communism caused by poverty, but disease, crime, juvenile delinquency, illiteracy, segments of the drug culture, riots and terrorism—all can be related to poverty conditions.

It is as though the soul of man were rioting against lack in this enlightened age, because the soul intuitively knows that man is supposed to be prosperous.

HOW TO OPEN YOUR MIND TO PROSPERITY

You can open your mind to prosperity by giving up that ridiculous idea that poverty is a Christian virtue, when it is nothing but a common vice. Poverty is definitely a sin, not a blessing.

As Charles Fillmore has declared in his book, *Prosperity*:[1]

The Father's desire for us is unlimited good, not merely the means of a meager existence. We cannot be very happy

---
1. Unity Books, (Unity Village, MO 64065, 1936).

if we are poor, and nobody needs to be poor. It is a sin to be poor.

There is nothing new about this idea. A century ago a Baptist minister named Dr. Russell Conwell became very famous because of one lecture, called *Acres of Diamonds*,[2] which he gave all over the United States.

Dr. Conwell made somewhere between eight million and twelve million dollars as he traveled about, over a fifty-year period, giving that one lecture—the proceeds of which he used to found Temple University in Philadelphia. As you study his famous prosperity lecture, you discover that he was trying to break down the listener's sense of guilt about becoming prosperous:

> I say you ought to be rich. You have no right to be poor. To live and not be rich is a misfortune, and it is doubly a misfortune because you could have been rich just as well as being poor.

You can open your mind to prosperity when you realize that through your study and application of the mental and spiritual laws of prosperity, you are not trying to make God give you anything. As the Bible promises, "All things are yours." (I Corinthians 3:21)

In the beginning, God created a lavish universe and then created spiritual man and placed him in this world of abundance, giving him dominion over it. (Genesis 1)

You are only trying to open your mind to receive your heritage of abundance bequeathed you from the beginning. You can begin opening your mind to this abundance by declaring often, "I AM THE RICH CHILD OF A LOVING FATHER, SO I DARE TO PROSPER!"

---

2. Russell Conwell, *Acres of Diamonds* (New York: Harper & Row, Publishers, Inc., 1915).

There once was a businessman who had his own simple formula for opening his mind to prosperity. When people asked, "How's business?" he had a standard reply, regardless of economic conditions of the moment: "Business is wonderful, because there's gold dust in the air." It always seemed so for that man. No matter what people about him were doing or saying, he prospered. His friends would say: "I don't understand it. Everything he touches turns to gold."

REPORTS OF THOSE WHO HAVE PROSPERED

In that first prosperity class in 1958, and in scores of classes I have conducted since that time, I have observed that as soon as people realize it is spiritually right, rather than spiritually wrong, for them to be prosperous, it is as though the windows of heaven were open to them!

Recent reports from people who opened their minds to prosperity include these:

A businesswoman doubled her financial income and then happily married a man of affluence, after having been widowed for ten years. A housewife accepted this great idea, and soon learned that her husband had just inherited a large portion of the company for which he worked. Another housewife watched her husband progress from one promotion to another in his engineering job. They inherited money, bought a new home and two new cars, and after having tried for a number of years were able to adopt several children. A young college professor obtained another degree and went on to a fine job at a much larger income at a state university.

A domestic worker demonstrated a six-week trip to Europe. A teacher was transferred out of an inharmonious department in her school to a far more congenial teaching position. One couple was able to buy a beautiful new home with no down payment. (The former owner *gave* them his eight thousand dollar equity!) One couple's two children both obtained college scholarships. A woman in the real-estate business got her broker's license and went into business for herself; another realtor made her first sale in a year!

Upon returning home from a prosperity lecture in Oklahoma City, a businesswoman answered her ringing telephone. It was a customer with a forty-dollar sale, at 12:30 p.m. on a Sunday. The next morning she was awakened by another ringing telephone—and another sale. This was quite a change from the "hard sell" approach to which she was accustomed.

A businessman walked out of a prosperity lecture, and on the way to his car found a twenty-dollar bill. Later that week, a raise he had been trying for months to obtain for his employees came through. After opening her mind to prosperity, a young widow was able to reduce her debts by $1,700 within three days!

PROSPERITY CAME TO ALL THOSE WHO HELPED WITH THE AUTHOR'S FIRST BOOK

You can open your mind to prosperity when you realize it pays to do so, right in the face of lack and limitation.

I started writing prosperity articles several decades ago, when I was living in one room. I felt foolish writing about prosperity, telling other people how to be prosperous, when I was living in just one room. But I realized that I must do something to open my mind to prosperity in order to get *out of* that room. It took me three years, but when I finally moved out, I found a lovely new home. (The move could have come sooner, had I known the complete prosperity formula given in this book.)

Opening your mind to prosperity in the face of lack can have dramatic effects on your life, too. This was brought to my attention by those around me while I was writing my first book. After typing the first half of the manuscript, my secretary resigned. She explained that as she had typed the manuscript she had used the ideas in it, and her husband had been prospered so much in his sales work that she no longer needed the job!

A second secretary was then employed to type the last half of the book. Before completing it, she also resigned. She explained that her husband had been out of work when she took the job, but that he now had the finest engineering job of his life—one which would take him to another state. She felt that the ideas in the book had turned the tide.

Finally, my housekeeper resigned. She had not seen the manuscript, but I had explained the laws of prosperity to her while writing about them, chapter by chapter. As she opened her mind to prosperity, she decided to do something she had long wished to do but had never quite had the courage—become a dressmaker. She said, "I am resigning as your housekeeper. Now would you like to hire me as your dressmaker?" She has prospered in that field of work ever since.

It was startling to lose two secretaries and a housekeeper while writing one book—just because they dared to open their minds.

But there's more: On the day that book was handed to my New York editor, he was sitting at his desk carefully perusing it, when another editor walked into his office and handed him some money. He was startled to hear that editor explain, "Some time ago you loaned me some lunch money. Until just a few moments ago, I had forgotten about it." My editor wrote me in triumph, "How's that for fast action from *The Dynamic Laws of Prosperity*?"

A REPORT FROM THE TYPESETTER
OF THIS BOOK

However, an even more updated report on the power of opening your mind to prosperity just came from the typesetter of this present book. From Hollywood, California, he wrote:

> I am the individual who had the personal pleasure of typesetting the revised version of *Open Your Mind to Prosperity* for your California publisher. This manuscript held my attention from the first paragraph to the last, and I feel much better both mentally and emotionally for having had the experience.
>
> *Open Your Mind to Prosperity* especially opened my mind to certain undeniable truths, most of which I knew in early life. But as I became more caught up in the grind of work and daily living, I had come to dismiss their importance.
>
> At one time in my life I had been an ardent believer in prayer. Yet I never knew how to effectively word my prayers, nor did I know that my prayers should be accompanied by visualization of the desired good. This book has brought home the art of dynamic prayer so concisely and succinctly. I had prayed for guidance in my life, but never dreamed it could come to me in this way—through typesetting *Open Your Mind to Prosperity*. I thought you should know.

And I, the author, thought you, the reader, should know!

THE TRUE DEFINITION OF PROSPERITY

You can open your mind to prosperity when you realize the true definition of the word: You are prosperous to the degree that you are experiencing peace, health, and plenty in your world.

Prosperity includes peace of mind: A businessman recently wrote, "The study of prosperity certainly does bring peace of mind. Since I took up this study, my wife has stopped griping at me, and my mother-in-law has started leaving me alone."

Prosperity includes harmony: A young musician who attended one of my prosperity classes had been out of work for a number of months. Immediately after the class, he got the finest job of his life. Later he wrote: "I had a nice surprise from my study. I took it up because I needed a job, which I quickly got. But at the time I employed prosperous thinking, my wife and I were estranged. We have now been reconciled and are happier than ever. Prosperity certainly includes peace and harmony."

Prosperity includes health: A housewife was taken by her husband to a prosperity lecture. This woman had been in pain for twelve years from a chronic ailment which drugs could temporarily alleviate but could not cure. When the drugs wore off, the pain returned.

On the way home from the lecture that night, she realized that for the first time in twelve years she was free of pain without using drugs. That was eight years ago. The pain has never returned.

This couple has gone on to financial success also, but their main prosperity demonstration was a physical healing.

Prosperity includes financial plenty: People sometimes reflect, "Since prosperity includes peace and health, prosperity is *more* than money alone."

True, but what's wrong with prosperity as money?

An important way to open your mind to prosperity is deliberately to open your mind to the idea that money is spiritual, that money is a part of your spiritual heritage.

THERE ARE MILLIONAIRES IN THE BIBLE!

It helps in opening your mind to prosperity when you realize that the great spiritual leaders of the Bible were prosperous people—many of them were literally millionaires.[3] They seemed to know that prosperity was a spiritual blessing and poverty was a curse.

In the first book of the Bible, we find four millionaires among the great Hebrew leaders: Abraham, Isaac, Jacob, and Joseph. The Bible vividly describes their wealth. We have often thought of Abraham as the father of the Hebrew people, which he was, but he was also a millionaire. The Scriptures declare that his substance was very great, and that the Lord "blessed (him) in all things." (Genesis 24:1)

When I first mentioned in a lecture that Abraham was a millionaire, a startled Texan asked, "If Abraham was a millionaire, how many oil wells did he have?"

I replied, "I don't know, but I'll find out." When I checked the Biblical description of Abraham's wealth, I could not locate a single oil well for him. But as I studied carefully the passages describing his wealth, one verse stood out: "Abraham was very rich in cattle, in silver, and in gold." (Genesis 13:2)

When I happily reported to that skeptical Texan that

---

3. See Catherine Ponder's series on "The Millionaires of the Bible," including *The Millionaires of Genesis, The Millionaire Moses* and *The Millionaire Joshua*, all published by DeVorss & Company, Marina del Rey, CA 90294.

Abraham had been a rich cattleman, he was so impressed that he insisted that Abraham's cattle were probably Longhorns originally from the Lone Star state! In spite of my protests, he left that lecture a very happy man.

THE BIBLE IS A PROSPERITY TEXTBOOK

You can open your mind to prosperity when you realize that the Bible is the greatest prosperity textbook ever written, and begin studying it from that standpoint. The Bible is filled with stories about bread and fish. This is marvelous prosperity symbolism: The bread symbolizes the substance of the universe, which we mold and shape with our thoughts and words of prosperity. The fish symbolize ideas of increase.

The word "gold" appears more than four hundred times in the Bible. There are between three thousand and four thousand promises in the Bible, many of them literal prosperity promises. (Some theologians claim there are nearer eight thousand such promises.)

Jesus' interest in prosperity is shown in the Lord's Prayer: "Give us this day our daily bread, and forgive us our debts, as we also have forgiven our debtors." (Matthew 6:11, 12) Many of Jesus' miracles were prosperity miracles, and many of His parables were prosperity parables.[4]

When Jesus said of the rich young ruler, "How hard it will be for those who trust in riches to enter the kingdom," it was because He knew that this rich man was possessed by his possessions rather than controlling them (Matthew 19:23, 24). *A spiritual consciousness of prosperity gives you control*

---

4. See *The Millionaire from Nazareth* by Catherine Ponder, published (1979) by DeVorss & Co., Marina del Rey, CA 90294.

over your possessions, rather than allowing your possessions to control you.

PROSPERITY IS NECESSARY FOR YOUR GROWTH

You can open your mind to prosperity when you realize that prosperity is a necessity for your spiritual growth, because prosperity gives you freedom to grow spiritually.

I once sat next to a doctor of chiropractic at a banquet where we were both guest speakers. This man told me how much the mental and spiritual approaches to prosperity had meant to him over the years. He described how he had gone from being a struggling young doctor who had nothing, to being a happy, affluent one who now has his own clinic, a large practice, a nice home, a fine family, cars, investments, property—even a private plane. He said this: "I am a far better doctor, a far better husband and parent, a far better citizen today because I am prosperous. I now have time to study Truth, to unfold spiritually in a way I never had before. *Everybody ought to be prosperous, because prosperity gives them freedom. Prosperity is a necessity for spiritual growth.*"

TRUE PROSPERITY HAS A SPIRITUAL BASIS

You can open your mind to prosperity by following Moses' advice to the Hebrews centuries ago: "You shall remember the Lord your God, for it is he who gives you power to get wealth." (Deuteronomy 8:18)

This is the prosperity secret of the ages: *God is the Source of your supply.* As long as you relate to the Source, you will be prosperous. It is when you turn from God as the Source and depend upon people and conditions for your prosperity that

you have financial problems. People and conditions are channels of your supply, to be sure, but God is the Source. Knowing this, you do not panic if the channel changes, but know to look to God as the Source for guidance and supply: "I DO NOT DEPEND UPON PERSONS OR CONDITIONS FOR MY PROSPERITY. GOD IS THE SOURCE OF MY PROSPERITY AND PROVIDES HIS OWN CHANNELS OF SUPPLY TO ME NOW."

Many years ago, when it seemed that people and conditions controlled my good, I found this passage in *Lessons in Truth*[5] helpful:

> No person or thing in the universe, no chain of circumstances, can by any possibility interpose itself between you and all joy—all good. You may think that something stands between you and your heart's desire, and so live with that desire unfulfilled, but it is not true. . . . Deny it, and you will find yourself free. . . . Then you will see the good flowing (to) you, and you will see clearly that nothing can stand between you and your own.

The statements I used at that time to help free me from the belief in personality's power to withhold my good, and to help me relate to God as the Source of my supply, were these:

"I CLEARLY SEE THAT NOTHING OR NO ONE CAN STAND BETWEEN ME AND MY OWN!"

"I DISSOLVE IN MY OWN MIND AND IN THE MINDS OF ALL OTHERS ANY IDEA THAT MY OWN CAN BE WITHHELD FROM ME. THAT WHICH IS FOR MY HIGHEST GOOD NOW COMES TO ME, AND IN MY CLEAR PERCEPTION OF TRUTH I WELCOME IT!"

"NOTHING CAN OPPOSE MY GOOD. NO ONE CAN OPPOSE MY GOOD. I NOW ACCOMPLISH GREAT THINGS WITH EASE."

---

5. H. Emilie Cady, (Unity Village, MO: Unity Books, 1894.)

"REFUSING TO CRITICIZE ANOTHER'S PROSPERITY, I TURN TO GOD, ASK HIS DIRECTION, AND I AM PROSPERED."

"LOVE ENVIETH NOT. THE PROSPERING TRUTH NOW SETS ME FREE."

"MY LIFE CANNOT BE LIMITED. MY FINANCIAL INCOME CANNOT BE LIMITED. CHRIST IN ME NOW FREES ME FROM ALL LIMITATION. I AM RICH IN MIND AND MANIFESTATION NOW."

"THE FORGIVING LOVE OF JESUS CHRIST NOW SETS ME FREE FROM ALL FINANCIAL MISTAKES OF THE PAST OR PRESENT. I FACE THE FUTURE WISE, FREE, AND UNAFRAID."

The Bible plainly shows that as long as the Hebrews recognized God as the Source of their supply and looked to Him for guidance, they prospered lavishly. It was when they turned from God and began to look to people and conditions for supply, during the time of Solomon, that the Hebrew nation divided financially and politically and went into exile.

THIS ATTITUDE IS PRACTICAL

Perhaps you are wondering, "But just how practical is this idea of looking to God as the Source of my supply?"

Another doctor said to me recently: "I never really prospered, though I worked hard trying, until I learned that prosperity has a spiritual basis. After I began to affirm daily that God was the Source of my supply—that I did not have to depend upon my patients or upon other people or upon economic conditions for my prosperity—I was able to build a new $100,000 clinic for my patients within eight months." He showed me pictures of his clinic, and it is truly beautiful.

This is a practical idea, that God is the Source of your prosperity and that your prosperity has a spiritual basis. When you open your mind to this freeing idea, you will begin to prosper.

You may be thinking: "Yes, but I know people who are not religious but are exceedingly prosperous. They do not recognize God as the Source of their supply."

Perhaps they are prosperous in a financial sense, but remember that true prosperity includes peace and health. What about their peace of mind and health of body?

SUMMARY

1. Prosperity is generated by mental and physical forces. To generate prosperity in your own life you must open your mind to it.

2. Give up the idea that poverty is a Christian virtue. Poverty is a sin, not a blessing.

3. You are not trying to make God give you anything. You are only opening your mind to receive the abundance God has promised you from the beginning.

4. It pays to open your mind to prosperity when you are faced with lack and limitations.

5. You are prosperous to the degree that you are experiencing peace, health, and plenty in your world. This is the true definition of prosperity.

6. Some of the great spiritual leaders of the Bible were prosperous. The Bible itself is a wonderful prosperity textbook, filled with prosperity stories, promises, and parables.

7. Prosperity is necessary for spiritual growth, in that it gives you the freedom to unfold spiritually, without having to worry about finances or the mundane side of life.

8. God is the Source of your supply, not people or conditions. Realizing that the basis of your prosperity is spiritual is a practical attitude and assures your financial success.

CLEANSE YOUR MIND
FOR PROSPERITY

— Chapter 2 —

Cleansing, or purification, is the first step in prosperity.

If people around the world knew the cleansing steps to prosperity and used them, they could revolutionize their lives for good!

The mystics had a three-point formula for success:

1. *Purification*, or cleansing.

2. *Illumination*, or receiving guidance on how to be prospered.

3. *Union* with God and His good.

These three steps to success are covered in this and the following chapters.

The Bible is filled with cleansing symbolism: sacrifice, renunciation, repentance. Even the "wailing wall" in Jerusalem is symbolic of the letting go of negative emotions that is necessary before prosperity can come.

The ancient Greeks observed rites of purification, and so must we!

Life is a constant purification process. If you try to bypass this cleansing process in your thoughts and feelings, you bypass your good, because you have not cleaned out your mind and emotions to receive the good you want.

Dr. Evelyn Underhill has explained: "The cleansing process forms a large part of our spiritual life. It is our own fault if we do not get purified in this life."

HOW TO CLEANSE YOUR MIND

You must get rid of what you do not want, to make way for what you do want. Substance (gold dust, mind power) does not flow easily into a cluttered, crowded situation. Substance does not flow easily into a cluttered, crowded mind. Substance does not flow easily into a cluttered, crowded, hate-filled emotional state.

You must begin to form a vacuum, in both outer and inner ways. Magnetic influences are transmitted perfectly through a vacuum. *By forming a vacuum, you become magnetic to your good!* I have seen it happen hundreds of times.

OUTER CLEANSING

Get rid of what you do not want in an outer way. Clean up, clean out the closets, desk drawers, house, car, office. Forming a vacuum in an outer way makes a believer out of your subconscious mind, which then goes to work in inner ways to manifest greater prosperity for you.

There has to be a release of the old to make way for the new. You can unblock your good by forming a vacuum.

A woman in Chicago heard about this vacuum law at a lecture one night, and decided to stay home from work the next day and clean out closets and drawers. Nothing happened when she cleaned out closets, but when she cleaned out dresser drawers she found thirty dollars she had tucked away and forgotten!

Another woman formed a vacuum by cleaning out her pocketbooks. In one, she found forty dollars she had forgotten.

A housewife formed a vacuum by getting rid of old, mismatched sheets in her linen closet. The next day, she received as a gift several new sets of sheets and pillow cases. But nothing happened until a vacuum had been formed to receive them.

A marvelous statement to use as you form a vacuum is: "I NOW LET GO WORN-OUT THINGS, WORN-OUT CONDITIONS, AND WORN-OUT RELATIONSHIPS. DIVINE ORDER IS NOW ESTABLISHED AND MAINTAINED IN ME AND IN MY WORLD."

PROSPERITY COMES QUICKLY WHEN A VACUUM IS FORMED

A musician in Southern California recently learned of the vacuum law of prosperity, and decided to invoke it by cleaning out his closet. Within twenty-four hours, three things happened:

Since he was a public school music teacher, he needed a summer job. As he cleaned out his closet, he got an idea for conducting music workshops in the summer sessions of colleges and universities. He made a telephone call to his New York agent, who liked the idea so much that within a matter of hours the agent had him booked at leading universities all over the United States, at an interesting income.

The second thing that happened was that another music teacher called him and said: "I'm getting more calls for free-lance (evening and weekend) work than I can handle. May I refer my overflow calls to you?''

This would give him a year-round second income, right in his own neighborhood.

The next morning after cleaning out his closet, he started driving to work on one of the famous California freeways. Along the way he spied a stalled car. Ordinarily he would have hurried on, but intuitively he felt guided to stop and offer assistance.

The owner of the stalled car was a woman wearing a white uniform. Upon examining her car, he said: ''I believe the engine is only overheated. I'll wait with you a few minutes and, if it doesn't start, I'll drive you to the nearest service station where you can get help.''

Noting the white uniform, he asked, ''Do you do domestic work?''

''Yes,'' was the reply.

''Do you have any days available?'' he queried.

''Yes, I have every other Thursday.''

''Good. If you'll come and work for my wife, you're hired.''

The teacher explained that for months they had tried to find help. Later he exclaimed excitedly, ''If all this happened just by cleaning out the closet, I can hardly wait to see what will happen when I clean out the garage!''

GIVE UP THE EXPENSIVE, EVEN THE NEW

In forming an outer vacuum, it is wise to give up the expensive as well as the inexpensive, if the expensive items involved are no longer of use to you.

I once had two lovely velvet suits which I hesitated to give up because they carried expensive labels. But every time I

looked at them hanging there, I realized that they no longer
fit me and were useless to me.

Finally I decided to give them up, even though they were
designer's clothes. Within less than a week, I received a letter from my sister saying: "I have a lovely velvet suit which
I bought while abroad. It is by far the most expensive gar-
ment I've ever owned, but I do not wear it. I am mailing it
to you in hope that you can use it in your lecture work."

Could I! It arrived just in time to accompany me on my
next trip, and its color even matched the auditorium in
which I spoke. Furthermore, it had cost even more than the
suits I had just given away.

That experience taught me that by giving up the expensive, one makes way for something even more beautiful to
come, without financial stress.

Dr. Ernest Wilson once gave this explanation: "All of
our loosing is not simply the loosing of so-called evil. We
must loose forms of the good as well. Good is seldom static.
It is progressive. It evolves. It changes. We must allow it to
be so. We must loose accustomed forms of good, when our
progress or that of someone else involved demands it. We
must not be afraid to trust that law that brought the good to
bring another that shall fulfill it. We must be willing to let
angels go, that archangels may come into our life. Loose
your good, hold it gently, free it readily."

Sometimes it is something new we need to release. Have
you ever bought something on impulse, only to realize later
that you did not need it? If so, instead of condemning yourself for having shopped impulsively, return it or otherwise
dispose of it. As you release it, you make way for the equivalent good to find its way to you.

I once bought a dinner dress on impulse, only to realize
later that it was not right for me. Soon after passing it on to
someone who delighted in it, my "personal shopper" called

to say that she had just received in stock several dinner dresses that seemed exactly right for me. Upon inspecting them, I found one that easily took the place of the one I had released. It was far more suitable.

A businessman recently said to me: "It also pays to get rid of that which doesn't work. I had long been haunted by a certain health problem which didn't clear up. One day I decided to form a vacuum by throwing out my medicine. I have not had an attack since."

CLEANSING THROUGH ORDER

You can cleanse your mind for prosperity by getting things in order generally. As you do so, affirm divine order.

God does not violate the orderly arrangement of events. Instead, He seems to withhold the next development until order is first established in the present situation, in the present state of mind.

A college professor's car was hit by a car driven by one of his students. The latter's insurance company did not properly respond to the claim. For two months this case dragged on, until the professor realized he had not affirmed divine order. When he got quiet and did so, he called again for another appointment with the insurance adjuster. This time the papers were ready for his signature, and a check was forthcoming.

Emerson spoke of "sublime order" rather than divine order. He wrote of man throwing himself "joyfully into the sublime order." A good affirmation for this is: "I AM IN DIVINE ORDER. I AM IN SUBLIME ORDER NOW."

When things seem inharmonious and out of order, don't rush about frantically trying to make them right in an outer way or trying to change other people and make them more orderly. Instead, remind yourself that lack of order first exists within you. If you can get your own thoughts and feelings orderly, the people, situations, and even the universe about you will respond in a more orderly way.

Two women were driving in a heavy rainstorm, when one of them remembered to affirm divine order. Quickly the fog lifted, the rains stopped, and they drove into clear weather.

Declare often, "THE INFLOW AND OUTFLOW OF EVERYTHING IN MY LIFE IS ESTABLISHED IN DIVINE ORDER. I AM PEACEFUL AND POISED."

MAKE YOUR ELIMINATION LIST

You can cleanse your mind for prosperity by writing out what you want eliminated from your life.

For many years I had made lists of what I wanted to manifest in my life. But one nagging problem did not clear up, and I could not understand why. Finally I read a little booklet which suggested that you write out what you want to eliminate from life first, and then list what you want to manifest. This, said the booklet, was the way to alter your life.

I tried this suggestion and it worked. In fact, it was amazing how quickly that nagging problem disappeared from my life, after I had battled with it for years, when I dared to write down that I wanted that problem eliminated.

INNER CLEANSING THROUGH RELEASE

The function of elimination is twofold: to eliminate error, and to expand your good. Elimination of something from your life is always an indication that something better is on the way! After writing about what you want eliminated, it is good to declare: "I LET GO AND TRUST."

When you are trying to achieve a result and it has not come, it is often because there is still something in mind, body, affairs, or relationships that you need to renounce, free, release, or eliminate. As long as you put off this elimination process, you put off results.

Every phase of life requires renunciation. Every advance means the rejection of something old. But elimination not only *takes* something from you, it *gives* something to you!

A businessman in Detroit said skeptically: "How does my subconscious mind know what to eliminate? It may eliminate the wrong thing."

The subconscious mind does not know. But the superconscious, or Christ Mind, *does* know what to eliminate and will work through both the conscious and subconscious activities of mind to properly eliminate from your world that which should be eliminated, when you call on the Christ consciousness to do so. This you can do through using decrees that declare the all-intelligent Christ Mind is doing the eliminating: "CHRIST IN ME IS MY RELEASING POWER. CHRIST IN ME IS MY FREEING POWER. CHRIST IN ME NOW FREES ME FROM ALL RESENTMENT OR ATTACHMENT TOWARD OR FROM PEOPLE, PLACES, OR THINGS OF THE PAST OR PRESENT. I NOW RELEASE EVERYTHING AND EVERYBODY OF THE PAST OR PRESENT THAT ARE NO LONGER PART OF THE DIVINE PLAN FOR MY LIFE. CHRIST IN ME MANIFESTS MY TRUE PLACE WITH THE TRUE PEOPLE AND THE TRUE PROSPERITY NOW."

I once used these statements of release at a time when I felt general dissatisfaction in my life but I did not know what needed to be released. I was soon offered a lovely apartment, in a complex where I had long wished to live. With the move came the release of old furniture and personal effects, from which I had wanted freedom. The new surroundings gave a new lease on life. Though I had not realized I needed the change and could have it just then, the Christ Mind had known it and arranged it when I used the foregoing statements of release. Divine Intelligence always knows what to do, and responds when we call on it.

CLEAN OUT YOUR LIFE

Along with cleaning out the closets, you must also clean out your life, if you wish to cleanse your mind for prosperity.

If you want to be prospered, be healed, and have your prayers answered, you must clean up and clean out your life. *It is useless to affirm benefits, protection, supply, guidance, and healing, if all the time you are doing things which you know are not right in the sight of God, and man.*

So often, when one first learns of the power of thought, he thinks he can use mind power to force other people to do what he wants them to do. He tries to plaster over his life with affirmations. He may even get temporary results, but those results will only be temporary unless they have been founded upon the right basis.

A lonely widow had led a life of emotional and moral compromise since the death of her husband, feeling that she had to settle for such an arrangement. Finally she realized that if she wished to remarry, she must clean up and clean out her life. It took at least six months to clear out various compromising relationships, but after she did there was a quiet period of trusting in God to show her the way. Within a year she happily married a fine man, whom she would not have met had she continued in her previous circle of acquaintances.

It is true that God (as divine law) withholds the next development until order is first established in the present situation. This woman proved that elimination is twofold, and that when she eliminated error from her life, the expanded good came.

For freedom in your relationships declare: "CHRIST IN ME NOW FREES ME FROM EVERYTHING AND EVERYBODY THAT ARE NO LONGER PART OF THE DIVINE PLAN FOR MY LIFE. EVERYTHING AND EVERYBODY THAT ARE NO LONGER PART OF THE DIVINE PLAN FOR MY LIFE NOW RELEASE ME. CHRIST IN ME REVEALS, UNFOLDS, AND MANIFESTS THE DIVINE PLAN OF MY LIFE NOW!"

CLEANSE YOUR MIND THROUGH
FORGIVENESS

Cleanse your mind for prosperity by practicing forgiveness. Many people are never permanently prospered, no matter what else they do, because they are holding grudges and negative feelings towards others. Until they get down to business and forgive, their prosperity does not come.

The word *forgive* means simply "to give up." Forgiveness is not an unpleasant, dramatic outer act in which you say "I am sorry" when you are not. Instead, forgiveness is a pleasant inner act that leaves you at peace with yourself and others.

It is good to give yourself a universal forgiveness treatment every day. This keeps your mind and emotions cleared of negative feelings that could block your good: "ALL THAT HAS OFFENDED ME, I FORGIVE. WITHIN AND WITHOUT, I FORGIVE. THINGS PAST, THINGS PRESENT, THINGS FUTURE I FORGIVE. I FORGIVE EVERYTHING AND EVERYBODY WHO CAN POSSIBLY NEED FORGIVENESS IN MY PAST AND PRESENT. I FORGIVE POSITIVELY EVERYONE. I AM FREE, AND ALL OTHERS ARE FREE, TOO. ALL THINGS ARE CLEARED UP BETWEEN US, NOW AND FOREVER."

THE MIRACULOUS RESULTS
OF FORGIVENESS

A schoolteacher had had a nervous breakdown, and her employer had told her she would never teach in his school system again. Even when her doctor finally approved her to return to work, her employer refused to place her. She and her husband had several children who would soon need to go to college. They also needed a larger home and a second car. This woman felt it imperative that she teach again.

When she learned of the prospering power of forgiveness, she realized that much ill feeling existed between her and her employer, and that forgiveness might be blocking her good. With a friend, she sat one afternoon and spoke words of forgiveness to her employer: "CHRIST IN YOU IS YOUR FORGIVING POWER. CHRIST IN YOU IS YOUR RELEASING POWER. CHRIST IN ME IS MY FORGIVING POWER. CHRIST IN ME IS MY RELEASING POWER. CHRIST IN ME IS MY PROSPERING POWER NOW."

Soon she learned that her employer had decided to go abroad for a year's study. The man who replaced him gladly employed her for substitute teaching again.

When you hold resentment toward someone or something, you are bound to that person or condition by an emotional link that is stronger than steel. The practice of forgiveness is the only way to dissolve that link and be free.

A businessman was delayed at the airport by bad weather reports. It was imperative that he make certain plane connections for an important business conference. Realizing that resentment blocks one's good, and that on the way to the airport he had been thinking resentfully of a competitor, he sat quietly in the waiting room and mentally said to his competitor: "THERE IS NO COMPETITION IN CHRIST, AND THERE IS NO COMPETITION BETWEEN US. THE FORGIVING LOVE

OF JESUS CHRIST FORGIVES AND RELEASES ANY ILL FEELING BETWEEN US, NOW AND FOREVER. WE BOTH GO FREE TO PROSPER.''

Soon after, he was informed by airline employees that the weather was clearing and a plane had arrived which would take him to his destination on time. It was as though his thoughts of resentment toward his competitor had literally held him at the airport until he forgave the other man.

Since the word *forgive* simply means to "give up," often the greatest way you can forgive others is simply to give up all ill thoughts about them, as well as all outer contact with them.

FORGIVENESS IS A CONSTANT PROCESS

Forgivenesss is a constant process. Whenever there is a block to my good, I ask: "Father, whom do I need to forgive? What experience or condition do I need to forgive? One person knowing and declaring words of forgiveness for everyone and everything in a situation can dissolve the problem, regardless of what others are doing or saying.

A woman attended a lecture on forgiveness and mentally spoke words of forgiveness to her husband, who had deserted her more than a decade before. She had not heard from him since. Within twenty-four hours, he telephoned her long distance, asking to see her again.

A noted marriage counselor has said that a good marriage requires a lot of forgiveness. We might paraphrase that and say that a good *life* requires a lot of forgiveness.

A disgruntled businesswoman attended a lecture on forgiveness, and at the close she said: "I feel great. I have just forgiven everyone I know." The lecturer suggested she continue speaking forth words of forgiveness each day, since forgiveness is a constant process. A few weeks later the woman returned and said: "I have been practicing forgiveness and I feel terrible. I just didn't know I hated so many people!"

If people daily practiced forgiveness, they would probably put most doctors, psychiatrists, psychologists, social workers, and loan companies out of business, because everyone would become healthy and prosperous.

HOW TO GET OTHERS TO FORGIVE YOU

Along with declaring that you forgive other people, declare that they also forgive you, because subconsciously they want to, whether they realize it or not. Everyone wants to be free of negative emotions, whether he consciously admits it or not.

Declare for others: "THE CHRIST IN YOU FORGIVES ME AND FREES ME. ALL THINGS ARE CLEARED UP BETWEEN US NOW AND FOREVER."

A mother had had a hectic time with her adolescent daughter, who finally eloped. The mother emotionally released her daughter, and declared that the daughter forgave her for all ill feeling between them. For some time it did not seem so, but she continued declaring it. In due time they developed a closer, freer relationship than ever before, but with freedom for all concerned.

About a year ago, in morning meditation, the name of a fellow worker kept coming to me and I had an uncomfortable feeling about him. Several months previously I had suggested a certain project to which he had objected, so I had dropped it. Each morning his name kept coming into my prayer time. I tried to dismiss it but continued to get an uncomfortable, unhappy feeling about him.

Finally I realized that perhaps there was a need of forgiveness between us, though I consciously held no ill will. When I spoke words of forgiveness to him, nothing changed. But when I began declaring that he forgave me, I felt the uncomfortable, unhappy feeling begin to pass away. Within three or four morning prayer sessions, the feeling had cleared up completely. A couple of weeks later, that worker contacted me and suggested that we go ahead with the project I had recommended several months previously. We did—and it proved to be one of the most successful we had ever carried out.

HOW TO GIVE AND RECEIVE EMOTIONAL RELEASE

A fine formula is to forgive your enemies and release your friends. Forgive the people you hate or resent. Release the people you love.

Loose your loved ones and let them go to their good. This may be the very thing you do not want to do. You feel that they need your encouragement, help, and understanding. But when you attempt to help them by keeping a possessive hold on them, they chafe so under your restraint that they are not free to love you as they otherwise would, and problems develop between you.

Remember this about release: *You never lose anything that still belongs to you by divine right, through the act of emotional release. Instead, you make way for your good to manifest in grander ways than ever before.*

Possessive, dominating people have all kinds of problems. Also, people who let themselves be possessed by others have all kinds of problems. There is a simple way to get and give freedom from possessiveness and domination, and that is simply by speaking words of release: "CHRIST IN ME NOW

FREES ME FROM ALL ATTACHMENT TOWARD OR FROM PEOPLE, PLACES, OR THINGS OF THE PAST OR PRESENT. CHRIST IN ME IS MY RELEASING POWER NOW.''

For others toward you: ''CHRIST IN YOU NOW FREES YOU FROM ALL ATTACHMENT TOWARD OR FROM PEOPLE, PLACES, OR THINGS OF THE PAST OR PRESENT. CHRIST IN YOU IS YOUR RELEASING POWER NOW.''

Once, when I had felt bound to people and circumstances, I used these statements—and soon found myself moved into lovely new surroundings, free of old memories and possessions. Several people quickly moved out of my life and found their good elsewhere. People, places, and things responded to those statements of release.

A possessive person often pours forth the substance of his thoughts and feelings into the life of someone else, so that he depletes himself emotionally and physically. Strong possessive emotional ties cause many of our problems—financial, health, and social.

Declare often: ''I NOW RELEASE AND AM RELEASED FROM EVERYTHING AND EVERYBODY THAT ARE NO LONGER PART OF THE DIVINE PLAN FOR MY LIFE. EVERYTHING AND EVERYBODY THAT ARE NO LONGER PART OF THE DIVINE PLAN FOR MY LIFE NOW RELEASE ME.''

A businesswoman had been divorced for twenty years. She wished to remarry and felt she had met the man of her dreams, but he would not propose. She waited patiently for several years.

Finally she talked over her problem with a friend, who said, ''There must be something from the past that needs to be forgiven and released.'' The friend then asked about her former husband. ''Oh, I have forgiven him for the unhappiness he caused me in the past, and he has remarried. But a strange thing happens. When my name is mentioned in his presence, he always becomes very negative and upset.''

Her friend said: "That may be the block. Let's declare here and now that he forgives and releases you forever."

These two women then sat quietly and called the former husband's name, declaring, "THE CHRIST IN YOU FORGIVES AND RELEASES ME NOW AND FOREVER."

Shortly thereafter, a stranger appeared in her office to inspect it. He became very interested in her personally, and began sending candy and flowers. She accepted his numerous dinner invitations. Her escort of several years' standing did not like this. In fact, he quickly proposed, and they got married. But nothing had happened until she spoke words of forgiveness and release from her former husband.

HOW TO GAIN RELEASE FROM TROUBLESOME SITUATIONS

It is also wise to speak words of release for situations or problems that you have struggled with and have been unable to resolve. These often respond quickly to this statement: "I RELEASE THIS SITUATION (THESE PEOPLE) TO THE PERFECT OUTWORKING OF THE CHRIST CONSCIOUSNESS NOW. I NOW LOOSE AND LET THEM GO COMPLETELY."

Once when I had struggled with a complex human relations problem for weeks to no avail, I released it to the Christ consciousness (which is the miracle consciousness) with the above words. This act gave me complete peace for the first time, and within a week the problem had quickly resolved itself in a way I could not have foreseen.

A housewife was moving and needed a maid to help with the packing, but could not locate one. One afternoon, after she had struggled with packing all day, she finally said: "Father, I release this packing and this move to You. I cannot handle it alone, so I place it in Your hands." Then she retired and took a nap. An hour later she was awakened by the ringing telephone. A voice on the line said: "This is Mary, your maid from two years ago. I suddenly had a feeling you might need me again. If so, I can come."

Someone has said, "Life is hard by the yard; by the inch, it's a cinch." Certainly when you daily practice forgiveness and release toward and from people, places, and things, you clear the channels for your good.

Declare often, "I AM IN RIGHT RELATIONSHIP WITH ALL PEOPLE AND ALL SITUATIONS NOW."

A woman's husband was in ill health, two of her children were struggling with unfortunate marriages, and she was struggling financially. Finally she said of all her problems: "I NOW GIVE THEM ALL TO GOD. OF MYSELF I CAN DO NOTHING." Within a matter of days, new supply came. Within a few weeks, her husband's alarming health problems began to subside. And within a month, her children had straightened out their marriages.

RELEASE HEALS

A businesswoman, in pain, limped into a prosperity lecture. There was a spur in her foot which her doctor had not been able to locate. He felt it would be better to let it work its way out rather than operate.

During the lecture she learned of the healing power of release, and later that evening spoke words releasing her health problems to the Father. Later in the night, she was awakened with a stab of pain from the affected foot. Examination revealed that the skin had opened, and the spur was breaking through. She was able to extricate it easily, and within a matter of hours she was walking normally again.

Words of release had brought literal release of an unwanted condition in her body.

SUMMARY

1. Cleansing or purification is the first step in prosperity. Without releasing mentally, emotionally, and in our visible world, there can be no permanent, satisfying prosperity.

2. In order to demonstrate true prosperity, you must get rid of what you do not want to make way for what you do want.

3. You can achieve this by forming an outer vacuum. By cleaning up and cleaning out the closets, drawers, file cabinets, desks, car, garage, etc., you make a believer out of your subconscious feeling nature, which then gets busy working with your conscious mind to cleanse your world for prosperity.

4. Form an outer vacuum also by affirming divine order and getting things in order generally: "I AM IN DIVINE ORDER. MY WORLD IS IN DIVINE ORDER NOW!"

5. Make a list of the things and conditions (even people) you want to eliminate from your life—both the tangibles and intangibles.

6. Along with cleaning out the closets, clean up and clean out your life. The skeletons in the closet have got to go, if you wish to be truly prospered.

7. Practice forgiveness toward others. It's easier than you think. Do this by speaking words of forgiveness.

8. Declare that others forgive. Subconsciously they want to.

9. When you forgive your enemies, release your friends.

You never lose anything through emotional release;
you make way for the highest good of all concerned to
manifest without possessive domination or undue personal attachment.

10. Declare that others forgive you. Words of release clear
up possessiveness and bondage when you decree that
the Christ in the situation and in the people involved is
the releasing power.

11. Also release situations or conditions you have been unable to resolve. This freedom often manifests in perfect
solutions quickly.

CREATE YOUR PROSPERITY MENTALLY FIRST—IN WRITING

Chapter 3

I once lectured in New Orleans on the subject: "You Can Have Everything." After the talk had begun, a businessman came rushing into the auditorium and said breathlessly to an usher, "I hope I'm not too late, because I'm here to get everything!"

There *is* a way you can have "everything"—and that is, by creating your good mentally first. It has been estimated that success may be as much as ninety-eight percent mental preparation and only two percent outer action. Jesus must have made a lot of mental preparation before feeding the five thousand, because He had them sit down in companies, look up, and give thanks first.

There are three basic ways in which you may create your prosperity mentally first:

1. In writing.
2. In pictures.
3. In words.

Several decades ago, when I began writing about prosperity, my son and I were living in one room. We might still be living in that one room if we had not begun creating our prosperity mentally first, by writing, picturing, and affirming it.

It was while we were living in that room that I learned of these three ways to create prosperity mentally. When my son and I began to use them, they worked. This convinced me that I must begin telling other people about them through my writing.

Stop looking to people or conditions for your prosperity. Start using these three simple prosperity techniques, as described in this and the following two chapters. As you do, you will create your prosperity mentally first. It will then overflow from the mental into the visible world as tangible results.

For several years my son and I had been living in one room which had been provided to us by the church I was serving. The trustees seemed satisfied that they were adequately providing for us. The financial situation of the church at that time certainly did not seem equal to providing us with any more elaborate living quarters. Yet our present ones were certainly insufficient. Several times I had timidly mentioned it, but the feeling had always been the same. The church had no funds to provide us with a manse—period. On that note the subject was always closed.

For many months I thought to myself resentfully, "Why doesn't somebody do something?"

Finally it occurred to me: "Why don't *you* do something? Why don't you create your prosperity mentally first?"

It was then that my young son and I decided to put into writing, picturing, and affirmation what we wanted—a church manse.

After writing out our list, placing pictures on a treasure

map, and beginning daily to speak forth the affirmation, "I AM BEAUTIFULLY AND APPROPRIATELY HOUSED WITH THE RICH SUBSTANCE OF GOD," an interesting thing happened. One day a man walked in, said he had just come into an inheritance, and wished to share the tithe from it with the church.

"How much is the tithing offering?" I asked.

"Eight thousand dollars," he replied.

"Great! There's the down payment on the new church manse."

Within a matter of days, a lovely house had been located in the most beautiful area of the city, and negotiations were quickly completed. Before we knew it, my son and I were moving into a new house with new furnishings. And just as quickly—perhaps as a bonus for all our prayer work—there appeared a fine housekeeper, who *insisted* she was going to work for us. She had read some of my writings and wanted to know more about prosperous thinking.

It seemed a miracle, since domestic help was at such a premium and hardly within my financial reach under ordinary circumstances. As she foresaw, her personal contact with prosperous thinking proved worthwhile. As mentioned in an earlier chapter, she later resigned as my housekeeper and did what she had always dreamed of doing: she became a dressmaker, a profession in which she is still in demand.

WHY YOU MUST CREATE YOUR PROSPERITY MENTALLY FIRST

Man is a spiritual and mental being, and lives from the inside out, through his mind.

As a loving Father, God is the source of your prosperity. This same Father has provided the substance of the universe (which I like to call "gold dust") that you can shape and form as prosperity. This substance is passive and impersonal, and waits for you to form it personally as you will.

You are master of the rich substance of the universe!

You claim your mastery and take hold of this substance, shaping, molding, and forming it with your definite, deliberate thoughts, words, and actions. As you become definite about prosperity, it becomes definite about you. *As you turn the great energy of your thinking upon ideas of plenty, you will have plenty, regardless of what people about you are saying or doing.*

It is through writing, picturing, and affirming prosperity that your thoughts, words, and actions begin working for you in happy, prosperous, productive ways.

Begin right now to get definite about prosperity, by sitting down and making a list of the good you want to experience in your life.

Emma Curtis Hopkins, a great Truth teacher at the turn of the century, once said: "Sit down at a certain time every day and write down on paper what your ideas of good are. You will find that such a practice will pin your mind down to the Truth, and you will demonstrate results."

Another eminent metaphysician, Dr. Emmet Fox, said that this is the way to "alter your life."

Remember this: If you just drift along without any decision or definite purpose, you become the helpless victim of circumstances. If your desires are not clear and definite, you become subject to the dominating personalities of people around you. The way to overcome difficulties is to set a goal in writing.

Have you ever at some point in your life become subject to the dominant personality of someone who knew what he wanted, and found yourself getting it for him? I have!

My son has usually known what he wanted, in detail. I once looked out the window and realized that the two sports cars I saw parked there were both the result of Richard's definite desires—not mine. I had never had any preference as to cars, but like most men, Richard had. The result was that not only was he driving a sports car equipped for racing —but so was I!

Furthermore, remember this:

If you do not know what you want and have no set purpose, your subconscious mind just produces a conglomeration of circumstances. This is why there is so much confusion in the lives of passive people. *Concentrate on one thing long enough, and you are sure to get it. Always have a definite goal in mind and write it down. Never let yourself drift—unless you want to end up with two race cars parked in your yard!*

There is a specific reason why you should get definite about what you want. The word *desire*, in its root, means "of the father." It is your Father's good pleasure to give you the kingdom, and it should be your good pleasure to receive it here and now.

How can you test these desires to be sure they are "of the Father?"

If the desires you have are only surface desires, they pass away, but if they are deep-seated desires for greater good that remain with you through thick and thin, they are from the Father. They are divine desires. You should *ex*press them *con*structively, rather than *sup*press them *de*structively.

Desire is God trying to give you greater good! Open your mind to receive it. Then get definite about that desire by writing it down, so that it can definitely manifest for you.

CHOICE IS A MAGIC WORD TO THE MIND

Choice produces results. Your mind constantly produces what you choose.

There is an ancient secret about the power of writing out
what you want, as mentioned in my book *The Prosperity
Secret of the Ages*:

> Your definite written words dissolve all obstacles and bar-
> riers on the visible and invisible planes of life. Your written
> words go out into the ethers of this universe to work through
> people, circumstances, and events, to open the way for your
> desired good to come to pass.

An artist proved this. She had an oil painting that had
not been sold, after having been on display for months. Finally she remembered to write out (on her list of things
desired) that this painting would sell quickly at the price she
was asking. She wrote this on her list on October 11. On
October 13 she received a long-distance call, informing her
of an art show in a nearby city. The caller was requesting
pictures from her to display at the show. She immediately
sent the oil painting that was on her list, and it sold (as
priced) the day the show opened.

Psychologists tell us that most things are done by choice;
that choice produces results, but that it is up to you to
choose what you want.

After I had written about this prosperity technique in my
book *The Dynamic Laws of Prosperity*, a businessman from
Philadelphia wrote me to verify the validity of this method.
He was once asked by a large corporation to give ninety-two
of their top executives a success course, for which the company paid him a large fee.

In this course, the executives were asked to write out the
things they wished to experience in life. The following results were reported:

> Miracles happened. Everyone was healed of health prob-
> lems, even of so-called "incurable" diseases. Out of ninety-

two men, all but two said they had gained vast good. All of these men got raises in pay of from two thousand dollars to twenty thousand dollars a year. Health problems, prosperity and personality problems, were all solved by using this list-making method.

THE PSYCHOLOGY OF POVERTY

Recently one of my readers,, who is a psychologist, explained that the poor are so caught up in their present problems that they do not plan ahead or think ahead. Also, they have great hostility and envy toward those who prosper. The poor are suspicious and resentful toward people who succeed in life.

What about you? Are you so wrapped up in problems of the past and the present that you have not taken time to plan for better things?

Are you hostile and envious of people around you who succeed? Do you criticize them? Have you made unkind remarks about them? How do you feel, and how do you react, when someone near you has a prayer answered or has some good thing happen? *Can you take it?*

Sometimes we are tested. Sometimes the good we desire in life seems to come to people around us first. If we can praise and give thanks for another's blessings, rather than be envious and jealous and critical, then we can be assured that those same blessings (or even greater ones) will come to us.

But if we make unkind remarks about, are hostile toward, or are envious of other people's blessings, we have failed the test. We stop similar blessings from getting through to us.

OVERCOMING ENVY

A statement you should use often to dissolve envy, hostility, jealousy, or criticism is this: "LOVE ENVIETH NOT. THE PROSPERING TRUTH HAS SET ME FREE TO PROSPER."

As you view the blessings that come to other people, remind yourself of this great truth: The longer your good is in coming, the greater it will be when it comes—so why envy anyone else his good? Indeed, when good things happen to other people, it is an indication that the same or even greater good can come to you!

Make your list. Think about what you really want. When good things begin happening to people around you, it is an indication that your good is near. You can draw it to you, and externalize it quickly, by writing it down.

An executive from Illinois once wrote me a long letter , in which he said:

> This business of writing a list of those things you feel you need in your life works. I have done just that and success became apparent almost instantly. Since then, everything I had on my list has come to me. Some of them were tremendous things, such as early retirement so that I might become a public speaker. I now am a lecturer for business groups at $250 per lecture.
>
> I also listed an adequate income, so that my life might continue normally as before retirement. Even such things as an expensive travel trailer, a fine motion picture camera, and other such items have come to me. *I have proved beyond all doubt that God intends us to have whatever we want that will advance our good on this earth.*

WHY THIS TECHNIQUE IS NECESSARY

You may be thinking, "Yes, but why are these simple techniques necessary from a spiritual standpoint?"

The soul of man must look outward as well as inward for balance. The soul is the blending area of the mind. You must balance the inner with the outer. That is why you are in a body on this earth plane, though you are a spiritual being functioning through a mind.

There is nothing more pathetic than to see those misguided persons who think they are too "advanced" or too "spiritual" to demonstrate the blessings of life in a practical way. Such individuals become confused and suffer all kinds of needless problems because they are not balanced.

Dare to do this simple thing: Make your list of what you really want—not what somebody else thinks you should have. As you make your list, dare to please only yourself, remembering that "the highest is the nearest."

Then keep your list private, a secret between you and your own indwelling Lord.

It is in this way that you *ex*press *con*structively—rather than *sup*press *de*structively—your desires, which are from the Father.

The very act of list-making clears your mind and your life. Recently I made a list of three things I thought I wanted to experience in my life. Six months later, when I looked at that list, I was amazed at how it had worked out.

The first item on my list had come to pass. It was by far the most important one. The second item had not come to pass, and events indicated that the answer to that desire was "no" for the time being. So I dismissed it in peace, feeling that it would manifest later, at the right time. As I looked at the third desire, I realized I had changed my mind completely and simply did not want it—and it had not taken place.

TESTING THIS METHOD

You can test this method by first using it on a daily basis.

A young insurance executive said: "I have bogged down. I now sell more than a million dollars' worth of insurance each year and am a member of the 'President's Club.' But I want to sell at least two million dollars' worth of insurance this next year, and go on up from there."

I suggested that he begin going to the office an hour earlier each morning, before his secretary arrived and the telephone started ringing. In that early morning hour, he was to write out a list of the things he wanted to accomplish that day. At the top of his daily list he was to write: "THE SUCCESS POWER OF JESUS CHRIST IS IN ABSOLUTE CONTROL OF THIS DAY, PRODUCING PERFECT RESULTS HERE AND NOW."

A week later he telephoned: "It works! I can hardly believe how much has been accomplished this week, easily and peacefully. In one day alone, I sold two fifty-thousand-dollar policies, and now I have an appointment to make the biggest sale of my life. I am well on the way to my two-million-dollar goal for this year."

He had outlined to me his five-year plan for success, which included an increase from two million dollars in sales to three million, four million and five million, with additional employees being added to his staff from time to time, I suggested that he work up the five-year plan on a poster board, and place it where he could look at it in his early-morning quiet time. This he had done.

ARE YOU WILLING TO TAKE WHAT
GOES WITH RESULTS?

After making your list, be ready and willing to change it, as the days pass and as your mind goes to work for you. Be flexible. Be adaptable. Be willing to expand and improve your list.

It is wise to make three lists:

1. What you want to eliminate from your life.
2. What you want to bring into your life.
3. What you are thankful for.

After making these lists, ask yourself the following questions:

First: Are these desires legal? Would they hurt anyone else if they came to pass? (There is an old saying, "The good of one is the good of all.")

Second: Are these desires emotionally right for you? Are you emotionally ready to accept them if they come?

Third: Are you willing to accept the responsibility that goes with having them?

Fourth: What are you going to give up to make room for them?

In his famous essay on *Compensation*,[1] Emerson explained, "For everything you gain, you lose something."

Every phase of life requires renunciation. Every advance means the rejection of something old.

A mother was anxious for her thirty-year-old son to marry. Though a well-educated and prosperous professional man, he was crippled. Both he and his mother feared he might never marry.

After taking some prosperity classes, she decided to write on her list the desire for her son to marry. Almost immediately, he met the girl of his dreams—who did not care that he was lame.

But his dream girl had been married before and had several children. This his mother had not counted on, nor was she emotionally prepared to cope with all that went with

---

1. From the *Writings of Ralph Waldo Emerson* (New York: Random House, Inc., 1940).

giving up her son. They had lived together for years, and
she had grown accustomed to his company—as well as his
financial help with her various interests.

When she realized what would happen if her son did
marry, she tore up her list—but it was too late. He was well
on the way to matrimony.

His mother never forgave the list-making method for
working so well! She refused to believe that elimination not
only *takes* something from you, but also *gives* something to
you—if you let it. Unfortunately, she never let it work in
this perfect way.

Buddha taught that each man is free, that he is the maker
of his own destiny through his choices, but that in making
his choices he must be willing to accept the consequences.

I recently looked at a list I made, month by month, for a
twelve-month period ten years ago. It was gratifying to
realize that everything I had asked for on those lists had
come to me—not always in the way I had anticipated, but
manifest they did. There were surprises that accompanied
some of them; even changes in residence and ministries, accompanied by moves to new parts of the country, were oc-
casioned by some items on the list.

After completing your list, you can protect your desires
by writing at the bottom: "THIS OR SOMETHING BETTER,
FATHER. LET YOUR UNLIMITED GOOD WILL BE DONE." Or, "I
RELEASE MY LIST TO THE PERFECT OUTWORKING OF THE
CHRIST CONSCIOUSNESS NOW."

This opens the way for your highest good to come to you.

SUMMARY

1. You can create your prosperity mentally first in writing.

2. The reason you should do so is this: if you just drift along without any definite purpose, you become the helpless victim of circumstances. If your desires are not definite, you become subject to the dominating personalities of people around you. The way to overcome difficulties is to set a goal in writing.

3. The psychology of the poor shows that they do not use this technique. They are so caught up in their present problems that they do not think ahead or plan ahead.

4. The poor usually feel much hostility and envy toward those who succeed in life.

5. Are you hostile or envious toward people around you who succeed? Can you take their success?

6. If you can praise and give thanks for another's blessings, you open the way for those same blessings— or greater ones—to come to you.

7. Write out what you really want, not what somebody else wants you to have.

8. It is wise to make three lists: what you want to eliminate from your life, what you want to manifest in your life, and what you're thankful for.

9. Ask yourself these questions: Are these desires spiritually sound? Are these desires emotionally right for me? Am I willing to accept the responsibility that goes with the fulfillment of these desires? What am I going to give up, to make room for them?

10. After making your list, keep quiet about it, bless it, and release its perfect outworking to the Father.

11. In this way you express constructively, rather than suppress destructively, your desires which are from the Father.

CREATE YOUR PROSPERITY MENTALLY FIRST— IN PICTURES

— Chapter 4 —

The second way to create your prosperity mentally is by picturing it.

The picturing power of the mind is now being re-discovered by psychologists, who say that imagination is one of our strongest mind powers. *Yet the picturing power of the mind is one of the oldest devices known to man for getting what he wants!*

Prehistoric man carved on the walls of his cave pictures of the food he hoped to obtain. He believed that, as he looked at those pictures often, an unseen Power would bring the food near him in the form of game, fish, or fowl.

Later, the ancient Egyptians used the picturing power of the mind in their tombs. As soon as a child of royalty was born, a tomb was started for him. On the walls of that tomb were painted pictures of his life, up to his death. The pictures showed all the experiences he could desire throughout his life: winning wars, living a happy, victorious life. The Egyptians expected these pictured events to come to pass in the life of the royal child.

Twenty-four hundred years ago, during the Golden Age of Greece, the cultured Grecians used this mental law and surrounded prospective mothers with beautiful pictures and statuary, in order that the unborn children might receive health and beauty from the mothers' mind-pictures. Prenatal psychologists are now rediscovering this technique.

THE POWER OF PICTURES

Instead of fighting problems, *picture* your way out of them.

The picturing power of the mind turns your thinking from ''I cannot have this'' or ''It will never happen to me'' to hope, belief, and finally to the mental acceptance that ''It can happen to me'' and ''It will happen to me.''

We talked in the previous chapter about the substance of the universe ''gold dust,'' which waits for us to mold it through our thoughts, words, and acts. We mold this substance into definite, tangible results through pictures.

We hasten our good by picturing it!

Generalities do not produce results, because they lack substance and power. Vague hopes and indefinite goals are not convincing to the mind, whereas a clearcut picture of the good we want activates people, places, and events to cooperate with our pictured desires.

A distraught housewife complained that her husband had been promised a job transfer and promotion for three years.

Because of company politics apparently he had been side-tracked. Pleading with the boss, prayer, and other methods simply had not worked.

A job with the company was open in this couple's home state, and they had requested a transfer to that job. Another couple was equally anxious to be transferred into the first couple's present location. In both instances, the requests for transfer had been turned down, and the job vacancies remained unfulfilled.

I suggested to this frustrated wife that she get busy picturing herself and her husband back in their home state, among relatives and friends; that she make out a "moving list" of all the things she would have to do before they could move; that she get travel folders with colorful pictures depicting her home state, and look at those folders often. In her meditations she was to live mentally in the desired situation, seeing her husband happy in his new job, and seeing them together as they enjoyed the tropical scenes of their home state.

She tried it, and for a number of weeks nothing happened. Then one day her husband received a phone call from the "big boss," who said he was moving them back to their home state, and moving the other couple who had requested it into her husband's present location. The boss had previously said no to these very requests!

This woman proved that one can picture a thing and bring it about rather than try to force it through in some outer way.

HOW PICTURING HEALS

A secretary was concerned over reports that her favorite young nephew would have to undergo brain surgery in a few days. She decided to make a "wheel of fortune" as a means of picturing him whole.

She used a file folder that she could carry with her through the day. In this folder, which served as her "wheel of fortune," she pasted recent pictures of her nephew, taken when he had been happy and well. Under his picture she wrote: "YOU EXPRESS RADIANT HEALTH."

On the inside of the folder, at the top, she wrote: "MIRACLE HEALINGS HAPPEN NOW, JUST AS IN BIBLE TIMES." Near his picture she wrote: "BILLY, YOU ARE SOUND IN MIND BODY, AND AFFAIRS." And at the bottom of the folder: "THANK YOU, GOD, FOR RESTORING BILLY."

Somewhere on her wheel of fortune, she taped these words: "A JOYFUL DAY IS AT HAND."

And it was. The next report she got was from Billy himself—a note in which he said that he felt great, had been released from the hospital without surgery, and had just returned from a hunting trip! Later she learned that when further tests had been made, prior to the scheduled surgery, the previously detected tumor had disappeared.

The interesting thing is that once this secretary made the wheel of fortune picturing her nephew whole, all concern about his condition left her. Picturing him whole had given her a wonderful sense of peace. Then came the good news from Billy himself.

HOW PICTURING WORKED FOR THE AUTHOR'S SON

At one time, I lectured extensively in Southern California and learned to love the area. Upon returning home to Texas, I talked with my son about the tropical beauty of Southern California, its strong metaphysical atmosphere, and its thriving prosperity; he became fascinated with the

possibility of living there. While still in high school, he
made a "wheel of fortune" for that purpose.

On this wheel of fortune, for which he used a big piece of
poster board, he placed pictures of himself surrounded by
pictures of Southern California: at the beach, playing golf
by a palm tree in the desert, wearing colorful tropical
clothes, with friends, driving on the freeways, and so forth.

When he made his California wheel of fortune, I assumed
it might work out for him to attend college in that state. For
many months he kept his pictured desires in his room,
where he viewed them nightly just before going to bed.
Finally he put the pictures away.

A couple of years later he decided to enlist in the Air
Force. When he came home on leave from basic training,
he said excitedly: "Guess what part of the country I've
been assigned to!"

"I have no idea."

"Of course you have. I'm going to Southern California!
I'm the only recruit, in hundreds from my basic training
class, who got that base."

His entire group had been scheduled to go to bases in the
North or Midwest, but before they reached his name on the
alphabetical listing, those bases were all filled. Along with
others, he waited for several hours while his commanding
officer tried to locate another base for him. When his orders
finally came, they read: "March Air Force Base, Riverside,
California."

That was only the beginning. Upon arriving in Southern
California, Richard was soon playing golf in the desert,
driving up and down the freeways, going to the beach, and
making new friends—all as pictured on his wheel of fortune
two to three years before.

One night six months later, he called me and said, "Do
you remember that sports car I had on my California wheel
of fortune—the pretty blue one?"

"Of course I do. And that was one item you never did get."

"That's why I'm calling—to tell you I'm now driving that car!"

"Not on an airman's income, you're not."

"Mother, think back to that wheel of fortune. Don't you remember that the blue sports car had a *blonde* in it? I'm dating that blonde, she has the blue sports car—and I'm driving it."

That one wheel of fortune has proved to me that imagination gives you the ability to rise above time and space, and overcome all limitations in your life!

In due time, my own pictures of Southern California brought results, and I have had the pleasure of living here for some years now.

WHY PICTURES MAY NOT WORK IMMEDIATELY

Many people become discouraged when a wheel of fortune does not work immediately. For vast changes that will have far-reaching effects, it usually takes time for the pictured good to be absorbed by the subconscious, feeling nature. When it is, those pictures begin materializing.

I once had a friend who lived in the Midwest. She and her husband wanted to move to Florida, and they made a wheel of fortune for that purpose. Within a year they were living in Florida, but it was four years before the home, the right jobs for both of them, their own boat, and new friends shown on their wheel of fortune appeared.

The pictured good comes to pass as fast as the subconscious mind can accept it. The pictured good may seem so different from past or present experiences that it takes time for the subconscious to absorb it. This is where persistence pays off.

On one of my lecture trips in Southern California I once

had the pleasure of dining with Dr. Ernest Wilson in his lovely home in the Hollywood hills. Founder of Christ Church, Unity, in Los Angeles, Dr. Wilson explained how the picturing power of the mind had worked for him to manifest his "hill house."

Years ago, when he first settled in Los Angeles, his office had been in the midtown area. From his desk he would look out the window to the Hollywood hills and think, "That is where I want to build a home and live some day." He had a number of homes in the interim but he persisted in holding to that pictured desire—and one day it materialized.

If the good you have pictured has not come about, it may be because you have cluttered your mind with too many pictures, or that you have stipulated too much for the present. As you clarify your desires and picture what you need most, this opens the way for it to come—often quickly.

A businesswoman needed a car. She also wished to remarry. She made a wheel of fortune showing a man driving a car. Nothing happened until she began to picture only the car she needed, without the man in it. Then a relative wrote to her, saying she wished to dispose of a car she owned and asked this woman to accept it as a gift. Since she had just entered a new profession which she was still learning, the time was not right for her to concentrate on a new marriage, too. Once she had clarified that in her mental pictures, what she needed quickly appeared.

NEW BUSINESS COMES THROUGH PICTURING IT

A housewife made a wheel of fortune for her husband. He had been working overtime, the year around, in a field of work that no longer interested him. On her wheel of fortune, she pictured a lovely swimming pool, large lawn, and terrace area. Also, they discussed their desire to have a business in which they would work only six months a year, rather than twelve.

Then came illness and financial setbacks, and they forgot their pictured desires temporarily. As he was regaining his health, the husband said he had no intention of returning to his eighteen-hour-a-day job, and now was the time to find that six-month-a-year employment.

Together they affirmed that a job he would enjoy was becoming available to him immediately. Three days later, his wife saw an ad in the paper about a business that was available for lease or sale. Investigation revealed that this business consisted of a "swim park," which would be open to the public for swimming and other recreational enjoyment six months a year. This was the type of business operation they had long wanted—and had pictured on their wheel of fortune.

Though he had no capital, the man was able to borrow the money needed to lease the business for a year, with an option to purchase later.

During the first year in the new business he lost five thousand dollars in its operation, yet felt he still wanted to buy it. When he was unable to come to terms with the owner, the business was sold to someone else. But instead of becoming discouraged, he felt so strongly that this was his divinely designed business that he said to his wife: "Honey, don't worry because someone else bought it. We have put many hours of love and work into its improvement, during the year we leased it, so it's really ours. I feel this so completely that I'll just continue picturing it as belonging to us." And he did.

Meanwhile he pictured the complete operation of the business, even to the employees and their duties. He made a list of the proper ways to render service, as well as im-

proved methods of operation. He also pictured himself own-
ing surrounding vacant property. He did all this at a time
when another man owned the business!

Then one day it happened. The new owner contacted
him, asked his advice, and confided that he wished to
dispose of the business in order to buy another one. Further
discussions brought them to financial terms, and the sale
was closed. The man who had pictured all this got out his
list of improvements and went into action, to hire the employees he had previously visualized.

Not only did this man get what he wanted through picturing, but everyone involved profited. The first owner sold
the property at a good profit. The second owner then dis-
posed of the property, and thereby was able to acquire the
property he really wanted. The man doing the picturing,
who became the third owner, was able to buy the property
at the price and on the terms that were right for him.

He was later able to buy surrounding property, as pictured. He has since had a thriving business which provided
for him and his family far more adequately than his
previous job had. He proved the power of pictures!

If you are wondering whether this man had the right to
picture this property as his when it belonged to someone
else—remember a great truth: The word *desire* means ''of
the Father.'' As you dare to picture God-given desires,
everyone involved is blessed and guided into his highest
good.

Also, remember that the action of the mind is to picture.
If you are not consciously picturing what you want in a constructive way, you are unconsciously picturing what you do
not want in a destructive way, and you continue to hold
problems to you. Deliberately picturing the good you want
is the way to overcome all problems.

CASUAL PICTURING BRINGS RESULTS

Casual but definite picturing also pays off, but usually not as fast.

A realtor who had learned of the power of picturing wanted to own certain duplex apartments which were for sale. Though he had been unable to arrange financing, he began spending some time every day in meditation, picturing himself as the owner of the apartments. While he was negotiating a loan on other properties one day, a wealthy benefactor learned of his desire to own the apartments and quickly agreed to arrange the financing. This amazed the realtor, who had not previously considered approaching this man, since the latter was financing so many of his other business deals.

As a little girl, I often longed for a birthstone ring in the shape of a heart (I was born on Valentine's Day), but I had never mentioned my desire to anyone, since my childhood had been far from affluent.

Several decades after my childhood picturing, I received a long distance call from a woman I had never seen. She said that after studying one of my books she had inherited a sizable estate. A part of the legacy was a mansion filled with valuable antiques, silver, and jewelry. She said that in appreciation for my writings she wished to share with me something from her inheritance. The thought had come often, she said, to give me a certain ring.

Rather timidly, she said, "You may not care for it because it is only an amethyst, which is not an expensive stone."

I found myself saying: "An amethyst? Why, I've wanted an amethyst for years. That's my birthstone!"

"Yes, but you might not want this one. It's different. It's in the shape of a heart."

While I tried to find words, she explained that the ring

had been part of a valuable art collection, which had come
down through the generations as a cherished possession.

Through the ethers, over many miles, and many years
later, a person I had never seen tuned in on my pictured
childhood desire and made me a gift of my rather unusual
wish—an amethyst ring in the shape of a heart. It was beautiful, and I have worn it as a reminder of the picturing
power of the mind.

WHAT ABOUT INHERITANCE OF PROSPERITY?

When I talk about people demonstrating prosperity
through inheritance, there are always some self-righteous
protests: "But I don't want to demonstrate prosperity
through inheritance."

Why not? If the soul of a man is going to pass on anyway,
why shouldn't you benefit from it? Someone will.

It is rather presumptuous to think your prayers for prosperity or your pictures of it would cause a person to die, just
so your desires could come true.

The spirit of man passes from this earth plane through
soul choice. He draws to him the circumstances and events
appropriate for his passing, according to his innermost
nature and accumulated karma. The most your pictures for
prosperity could do would be to influence him to arrange
his financial affairs to benefit you at the time when he
passed on. But to think your desires for greater good would
take him from this earth plane, just to benefit you, is rather
far-fetched.

A good rule of thought to follow is simply to picture your
desired good, then let it come as, when, and through whom
it may. If the most natural, normal channel is an inheritance, then accept it.

A businesswoman learned of the picturing power of the mind and decided to use it to demonstrate $10,000. Every day for a little while she took a $10,000 bill in "play money," held it in her hand, looked at it, and declared, "TEN THOUSAND DOLLARS NOW COMES TO ME IN GOD'S OWN WAY, FOR MY PERSONAL USE, AND I USE IT WISELY."

She continued this picturing process daily for several months. One day her attorney informed her that she had inherited $10,700 from her mother's estate. She has since gone on to increased prosperity through a better job, but that $10,000 proved a tremendous blessing to her. She certainly has not condemned herself for the way in which it manifested. She pictured it, claimed it, and then the way opened for it to manifest in "God's own way," which in this instance was through inheritance.

PICTURING RESOLVES FAMILY PROBLEMS

You can picture good for others and help bring it about. Some people are afraid to do this, though they think nothing of continuing to picture problems for others through their fears, worry, and negative talk.

You are constantly picturing, for yourself and for others, either something good or something bad. How much more constructive it is deliberately to picture something good for others, rather than to continue picturing problems for them.

The parents of a young girl were very concerned because she had vowed she would not go to college. Her steady date was a high-school dropout. The situation looked bleak until her mother made a wheel of fortune, picturing her daughter's happy, normal future.

On the wheel she placed pictures of a well-adjusted girl,

happily attending college. She even dared to stipulate in words and pictures that her daughter would successfully finish college. There were pictures of college friends, too.

Saying nothing to anyone, the mother began daily to look at the pictures, and she immediately relaxed and felt better about her daughter. Within a matter of weeks the daughter, then a high-school senior, announced she had decided to attend college for one year, "just to see what it would be like," she explained. The mother smiled with a sigh of relief.

During her first year away at school, the girl's world expanded so much that she lost interest in her hometown beau, the dropout, who then dropped out of her life.

Toward the end of her freshman year, she annnounced she wished to continue in college the following year—and did so. While a sophomore she met a new boy friend, and they were soon speaking of marriage. In their senior year, well on the way to graduation and with future jobs assured, they married. The husband is a high school coach, and the wife teaches in the same school.

All this happened thanks to a mother who knew the power of picturing—and did something constructive about it.

PICTURES BRING WORLD TRAVEL

In chatting with a prominent church layman who had just returned from a trip around the world, I commented on his marvelous "travel consciousness."

He said: "It's all my wife's fault. She made a wheel of fortune for traveling around the world, and placed it on the bedroom door where we would see it every day. That was several years ago, and we've already been around the world three times. We don't have that kind of money but we have friends who do. They keep inviting us along as their guests, just to keep them company. If my wife doesn't remove that wheel of fortune from the bedroom door, we'll probably just continue going around the world." Recently this couple took another trip abroad.

In modern times we have heard much about improving our "image." Picturing the kind of life you truly wish to live is a great way to improve your image and help it manifest.

Cities often use picturing power for "master planning." They employ specialists whom they call master planners. A news bulletin recently stated that a certain city had been refused federal funds to assist its expansion, because this city had no "master plan."

One might wonder how often many of us have been refused the funds, the aid we needed from the realm of universal substance, because we had no master plan through which mind power, gold dust, or substance could manifest as greater good in our life.

As we search the pages of history, we find that many great people unconsciously used some of these creative laws of prosperity. Napoleon kept a large map before him, with colored flags indicating the various moves he planned for his armies to make, months in advance. He also wrote down his plans and desires. Historians say that he dictated in detail the order and length of the marches, the meeting places of the two armies, the attack, the movements of the enemy, and even the blunders he expected the enemy to make—two months before it happened, and six or seven hundreds miles away from the scene.

WHEN IMAGING DOES NOT SEEM TO WORK

An unmarried woman recently wrote, "I have been imaging a husband for myself for over a year, but nothing has happened." She described in great detail the ways she had gone about this picturing process. She also wrote of several broken romances.

Perhaps there was a need for forgiveness and release in connection with those broken romances. I also had the feeling that the young woman was working too hard mentally, so that she was repelling rather than attracting her desires. She seemed to be trying mentally to force results.

After making your wheel of fortune, work with it daily for a time. When you get a sense of peace about it or lose interest in it, that usually indicates you are ready to release your desires and let them work out. My son has often said, "When I put my wheel of fortune in the basement, that's when it works."

There comes a time to observe a Sabbath. Just relax, giving your desired good the "light touch." This is the time to "let go and trust," or to "let go and let God."

Once the work is done on the mental plane, you can be assured your pictured good will manifest on the outer plane just as soon as the time, people, and events have arranged themselves accordingly. Such details are not up to you. This is the time to remind yourself that you have only to picture a thing and bring it through, rather than try to reason it through or force results.

SUGGESTIONS FOR MAKING A WHEEL OF FORTUNE

An engineer in Alabama designed a wheel of fortune which worked so well for him that he went from a mediocre job in the Deep South to a multimillion-dollar construction job in the Midwest. He used a large piece of poster board, outlining a circle on it which he divided for the various departments of his life: financial, job, family, health, etc. In each segment he placed pictures of the good he wished in that phase of his life.

Here are some further suggestions:

First: Keep quiet about your pictures. Do not discuss them or try to convince others to try this method. The words *secret* and *sacred* have the same root meaning. What is sacred should be secret.

Second: Use big, colorful poster boards, if you want big, beautiful, colorful results in your life.

A college professor made a small, crowded, drab, colorless wheel of fortune for travel abroad—and it worked. He had a crowded, drab, colorless trip.

Third: Use definite colors for definite results desired. According to the ancient science of color, you should use:

Green or gold poster boards for financial wheels of fortune, for job and career success.

Yellow or white for increased spiritual understanding.

Blue for intellectual accomplishments, such as writing a book, or finishing studies toward a degree.

Orange or bright yellow for health, energy, a more vital life.

Pink, rose, or warm red for love, harmony, marriage, happiness in human relationships.

Color is important because color impresses the subconscious mind much faster than black and white can. Whether or not you follow the foregoing ancient color chart, be sure to use colored poster board, always a color that appeals to you emotionally.

Fourth: Use colored pictures, rather than black and white ones, on your colored poster board. A recent comment was: "Now I know why my pictured good took so long to appear. I had used black and white pictures and backgrounds, rather than colored ones."

Fifth: Do not clutter your board, unless you want cluttered results. Make several boards, for various phases of your life.

A housewife recently exclaimed: "Now I know why our house is so crowded. We placed a small crowded house on our wheel of fortune, and we got just that."

Sixth: On your financial poster board, put money, not just the things you want. Otherwise you may get the things, plus indebtedness! (You can use "play money," also checks, on the board.)

Seventh: Place a spiritual symbol on your poster board, such as a picture of the Christ or the Bible. This gives your desires a spiritual protection, and opens the way for what you have pictured (or something better) to come to you.

Eighth: View your wheel of fortune every day, preferably just before sleeping. The more often you view your pictured desires, the quicker results will come.

SUMMARY

1. The second way to create your prosperity mentally is by picturing it.

2. The picturing power of the mind is one of the oldest devices known to man for getting what he wants.

3. Instead of fighting problems, picture your way out of them.

4. The picturing power of the mind turns your thinking from "I cannot have this," or "it will never happen to me," to hope, belief, and finally to mental acceptance that "it can happen to me," and "it will happen to me."

5. You can hasten your good by picturing it. You can help others by picturing the good for them.

6. Generalities do not produce results, because they lack substance and power. Vague hopes and indefinite goals are not convincing to the mind, whereas a clearcut picture of the good you want activates people, places, and events to cooperate with your pictured desires.

7. You can picture your way to increased prosperity, health, family harmony—even world travel.

8. You can picture a thing and bring it about rather than trying to reason it through or force results.

CREATE YOUR PROSPERITY MENTALLY FIRST—THROUGH THE SPOKEN WORD

— Chapter 5 —

The third way to create your prosperity mentally is by speaking the word of prosperity.

Florence Scovil Shinn once said, "Any man who does not know the power of the spoken word is behind the times." I agree.

By first listing your desires and then picturing them, you create your good on the invisible plane. You gather the substance ("gold dust") of the universe together on the invisible plane. But it is through the spoken word of prosperity that your words then move on that invisible substance, form it as definite results, and give it birth in the visible world.

The words *utter* and *outer* have similar roots. What you utter becomes outer in your world!

Christmas was coming, and a certain woman needed more money. She consulted a friend, who said, "Just affirm that you have 'plenty to share and to spare.'"

She did. That Christmas, people kept giving her fruit-cakes. She had plenty of fruitcakes to share and to spare, but no money.

If you would have more prosperity come to you, speak definite words that will bring it. Do not expect a general affirmation to produce a specific result.

The great people of the Bible knew the power of the spoken word, and they dared to get definite about prosperity in their words. Jesus affirmed, "Give us this day our daily bread." (Matthew 6:11)

It has been estimated that the spoken word of prosperity can speed up results by as much as eighty percent. I believe it!

A businessman had been jobless for four years, was fifty-five years of age, and had been informed he was "too old" to get another job. He had studied metaphysics for thirty years, but had been unsuccessful in applying it to his job situation.

When asked about the affirmation he was using, he replied, "I have been reading inspirational books and attending church services, but haven't used any specific affirmation decrees."

He was reminded that for every fifteen minutes of inspirational study, he should spend at least five minutes speaking affirmations. He decided to try it. He daily affirmed aloud, "I AM A DIVINE IDEA IN THE MIND OF GOD, AND I AM NOW GUIDED INTO MY TRUE PLACE WITH THE TRUE PEOPLE AND WITH THE TRUE PROSPERITY."

Within a short time, one of the many jobs he had applied for opened to him, and he became manager of the South American division of a large U.S. company. He later wrote:

I can attest to the fact that spoken decrees get your prayers answered. Prosperity affirmations turned the tide from failure to success for me when I had been out of work

for four years, was heavily in debt, and when just reading
inspirational books had not produced results.

Reading *about* prosperity isn't enough. *It is the spoken word
of abundance that gathers it to you.*

PROSPERITY AFFIRMATIONS THAT WORK

A prosperity affirmation that increased one man's annual
income to four times its previous level was this: "I HAVE A
LARGE, STEADY, DEPENDABLE, PERMANENT FINANCIAL INCOME
NOW."

A teacher who needed extra income began affirming "I
GIVE THANKS FOR A QUICK AND SUBSTANTIAL INCREASE IN MY
FINANCIAL INCOME NOW." After one session of verbal affirmation, she got the idea to apply at a certain fashionable
clothing store for a part-time job, one night a week and
Saturdays. They hired her. Not only has she enjoyed the increased income, but the job—working with beautiful mer-
chandise in beautiful surroundings—has given her a change
of pace, and she now looks forward to both jobs with
pleasure.

A businessman went from a $12,000-a-year job to
$25,000 a year, within six weeks from the time he began af-
firming, "I AM SURROUNDED BY DIVINE SUBSTANCE AND THIS
DIVINE SUBSTANCE NOW MANIFESTS FOR ME IN RICH APPROPRI-
ATE FORM."

An affirmation that has often opened new channels of
supply for many is, "I TRUST THE UNIVERSAL SPIRIT OF PROS-
PERITY TO PROVIDE RICHLY FOR ME NOW."

A couple moved from one town to another. In the process
of moving, some furniture was damaged. The insurance
company which was supposed to cover the loss would not

even send a representative out to check on the damage. The couple finally resorted to writing the insurance commissioner, but this brought no action either.

One day after attending a prosperity lecture, they began affirming these words: "I TRUST IN THEE, O GOD, AND THY RIGHTEOUS LAW. I KNOW THAT MY OWN WILL COME TO ME, AND I REST IN CONFIDENCE AND PEACE."

Shortly thereafter, a representative from the insurance company telephoned them long distance, said he was sorry about the "oversight," and offered them a settlement.

WHY PROSPERITY AFFIRMATIONS ARE SO POWERFUL

The ancients knew why. They knew about the dynamics of sound. They knew that every spoken word has tremendous power, and that by certain arrangement of words, tremendous vibratory forces can be set up in the invisible, profoundly affecting substance and producing results.

You can work wonders in your life by affirming prosperity out loud for just five minutes a day!

A widow who went "from rags to riches" within twenty years attributed her success to the daily use of one prosperity decree: "GOD IS MY SUPPLY AND MY UNLIMITED ABUNDANCE OF EVERYTHING NOW." After beginning to affirm this, she went into business on a shoestring, and for a time had to pray for her daily supply.

Once when she desperately needed one hundred dollars, she walked the floor and spoke her prosperity affirmation aloud. As she was doing so, her secretary opened a file cabinet and found five old twenty-dollar bills, "hidden" in an order pad!

Another time, when she was affirming God as her unlimited abundance in an attempt to meet the payroll for her employees, a stranger walked into her store and offered to buy a piece of property he said she owned down the street.

She exclaimed that she only wished she did own that piece of property! When the stranger explained that her father (now deceased) had bought the property for her many years previously, her attorney verified it. The businesswoman then sold the piece of property that, a few hours before she had not even realized she owned, met her payroll, and had an abundance left over.

HOW PROSPERITY AFFIRMATIONS HAVE ENRICHED OTHERS

During the depression years, a housewife daily gathered her little daughters around the kitchen table, where they said prosperity decrees for the head of the house, who was out of work: "YOU HAVE A WONDERFUL JOB, WITH WONDERFUL PAY. YOU RENDER A WONDERFUL SERVICE IN A WONDERFUL WAY."

It worked. At the depth of the depression, her husband was offered a job in the bonding business, if he could raise just twenty-five dollars to get started. He "raided the sugar bowl" and went into business. His wife recently stated that they were now worth $250,000.

She commented: "That twenty-five dollars became a quarter of a million dollars because I continued to speak prosperity decrees daily, over the years." Furthermore, the daughters who helped her say the original prosperity affirmation are now all married to prosperous men and are leading busy, happy lives.

Be definite in your words about prosperity, if you want prosperity to be definite about you!

By using prosperity affirmations, you are not trying to make God give you anything. You are only trying to open your mind to receive the abundance He has already given you!

There once was an engineer in England who heard of spiritual healing, and decided to investigate it in order to expose it as a hoax. He quickly discovered it was no hoax, became fascinated with the study of "New Thought," and later left his engineering profession to become a metaphysician.

He made the change rather suddenly, and so was in need of money. He decided to spend fifteen minutes a day, for one year, affirming prosperity, ease, money, and comfort.

Within a few weeks he had demonstrated prosperity—to the extent that he never had to worry about money again. Nevertheless, he continued daily to speak the word for prosperity, as planned.

THE AUTHOR'S EXPERIENCES WITH AFFIRMATIONS

Over the years, the power of the spoken word has proved priceless to those who have used it.

My first book got into print as a result of affirmations. During the recession of 1958, by request I taught a class on the spiritual and mental laws of prosperity. The people in my ministry were helped so much by it that they asked me to put the material from that class into a book. Never having written a book, I felt I had neither the time nor the talent for such a project and said so.

However, one businessman in that class felt so strongly that I should write such a book that he offered to meet with me for an hour every morning at the church, to pray affirmatively about it. At the time we started making affirmations, I had neither a book, a title, a publisher, nor any experience for such a task, so it seemed a fantastic prayer project.

Nevertheless, as we began daily to use decrees, the whole format for the book unfolded to me in prayer, even to the chapter headings. As we prayed for a name for the book, a stockbroker in the prosperity class suggested an appropriate title: *The Dynamic Laws of Prosperity*.

Now we needed a publisher. Under the circumstances, it seemed preposterous that I, an unknown writer, could just "break into print" successfully. But as we prayed affirmatively, decreeing that the God-appointed publisher would appear, an amazing thing happened: A man in the public relations business, who had been helped by the class instruction, walked into my office one day and said: "Your prosperity class has helped me and my business so much that I want to do something for you. What can I do?"

When I explained my writing project, he said: "I have a friend in New York who is a well-known literary agent. Ordinarily she does not take on unknown writers, but I will ask her about representing you." The result was that I soon had an agent, and a publisher.

Thus the book, its title, and its publisher all came after the power of affirmation was employed. Then, as we affirmed that I would have time to write the book amid a heavy schedule of church work, somehow, in the middle of the night and at odd moments, the book was written. As the book was being completed, I was guided to marry an English professor. Later his fine editing helped to make the book a best seller.

Affirmative prayer did a thorough job of providing me with all that was needed to launch my book into print! Yet the only "contact" or "influence" I had was that of affirmative prayer!

SPOKEN WORDS QUICKLY TURN THE TIDE

Often the casual word of success, as expressed in general conversation, produces tremendous results quickly.

A discouraged woman telephoned a church secretary, saying she wanted to attend a prosperity lecture being given that evening. "But I cannot attend, because I have no transportation."

Quickly the secretary declared: "Of course you will have transportation, and I'll look forward to seeing you at the lecture."

A few minutes later, the woman called back to report happily: "You were right. I will have perfect transportation. My brother just dropped by for a visit, and said he would be happy to attend the lecture with me!

Because of the power of words, whatever a person voices he begins to attract.

A group of fifty people had been studying Truth for some time. They were meeting in rented quarters for their church services, and it was not a satisfactory arrangement.

Then came a change of ministers, and the new minister knew about the power of words—knew that whatever a person voices he begins to attract. At the close of each church service, this minister conducted a short meditation, in which he described their new church and its quick and perfect manifestation. When he first began describing the new church in meditation, nobody paid any attention. They kept thinking, "There's no way." But as he persisted regardless of appearances, a group of men in the church asked to investigate the possibilities of a church loan from a reputable mortgage company.

The mortgage company assured them of their interest, and in a matter of months property had been located, plans drawn, and a building program undertaken. The minister continued speaking the word for their new church, week after week. Soon after moving into the lovely new building, attendance had grown from the original fifty to almost three hundred people.

They proved the power of speaking the word as one wants things to be, regardless of conditions. The spoken word is so powerful that it begins to change conditions to conform to what has been spoken.

The law of demonstration demands that what you desire to be and to do, you must declare you are and can do. *Many a person has struggled needlesssly for years with the problem of supply, when his spoken word would have quickly released the necessary funds to him.*

YOUR SECRET TEXT FOR PROSPERITY

The ancient people felt that it was good to have a secret word, motto, or text which they could hold to in time of trial or strain. They felt that this "secret text" would rearrange their affairs and bring them through to victory.

Among the secret texts they held to in times of trouble were "Jehovah" or "*I AM*" in Old Testament times, and "Jesus Christ" in New Testament times.

I first become aware of the prospering power released through dwelling upon the name *Jesus Christ* when I heard of Dr. Ernest Wilson's experiences many years ago. We have often thought of Jesus as the great Healer, and He was. But He also used the mental and spiritual laws of prosperity, as evidenced by many of His prosperity miracles.

Jesus Christ was the master Teacher of prosperity. No person's name ever stood for such colossal achievement as the name of Jesus

Christ. This is power for colossal achievement, along all lines, to those people who dwell upon that name today.[1]

This came to my attention when Dr. Wilson related how, during the depression, he began nightly to contemplate the Christ in his meditations. At that time he was reasonably successful. He was editor-in-chief of the Unity publications, was giving a number of radio talks each week, conducting a weekly class in Kansas City, as well as delivering a Sunday night lecture, and teaching a class in Sunday school.

Nevertheless, he became restless with a "divine discontent." As he nightly contemplated the Christ, not only did unusual spiritual growth take place, but prosperity and success opened to him in a big way. The weekly class he had been conducting grew from four hundred to fourteen hundred. The Sunday-night lecture grew in attendance from four hundred to nine hundred. The Sunday school class grew from seventy to three hundred.

As he continued to dwell on the Christ in nightly meditations, he began to write and lecture extensively. A few years later he went to Los Angeles, where he founded Christ Church, Unity. For many years under his leadership, it was one of the world's largest metaphysical churches.

Charles Fillmore discovered the prospering power that is released in the name *Jesus Christ.* He wrote in his book *Prosperity*:[2]

> The mightiest vibration is set up by speaking the name *Jesus Christ.* This is the name . . . above all names, holding

---

1. See Catherine Ponder's *Dynamic Laws of Healing* (Chapter 8) and *Pray and Grow Rich* (Chapter 7). Both chapters deal with the miracle consciousness of Jesus Christ.
2. Charles Fillmore, *Prosperity* (Unity Village, MO: Unity Books, 1936).

in itself all power in heaven and in earth. It is the Name that has power to mold the universal substance. It is one with the Father-Mother substance, and when spoken it sets forces into activity that bring results.

THIS SECRET TEXT HELPED THE AUTHOR

Since I have discovered this "secret text" for prosperity, I have found that my biggest demonstrations of good come after I use Jesus Christ affirmations.

I recall once sitting in my church study in the early morning hours, planning my work for that day and realizing there were not enough people to help with it. I needed a fast typist to do some special work that had to be done. I began decreeing, "JESUS CHRIST NOW MANIFESTS THE PERFECT TYPIST TO PRODUCE THIS WORK QUICKLY," and wrote out those words on a card which I propped up against the telephone.

About an hour later, a woman came running—not walking—into my study. Breathlessly she said: "Here I am. While having breakfast, I suddenly had the feeling you needed me. What shall I do?"

"Can you type?" I asked, trying to sound casual.

"Can I! Before marrying my husband, I was his secretary, and I'm one of the fastest typists in this town." Within a few hours she had done—as a gift, free of charge—what would have taken the average typist several days to accomplish.

In another instance, I had tried for weeks to get a repairman to my apartment. He had promised to come, but had not. The situation was getting critical because guests were scheduled to arrive. In praying about it again one night, I found myself decreeing, "JESUS CHRIST IS HERE, MAKING THE PERFECT REPAIRS NOW." Later I wrote down those words in my book of affirmations. A great sense of peace descended over me, and I released the matter.

The next morning quite early there was a knock at the door, and the repairman quickly did the work he had promised to do weeks before!

HOW OTHERS HAVE BEEN HELPED BY
THIS SECRET TEXT

A businessman was very discouraged. He had a drinking problem which for some time he had been able to curb, but the strong desire for drink had come to him again. Also he had health problems, and trouble was brewing in his marriage. His sales were down, so financial difficulties, too, had ensued.

Finally he sought the advice of a friend, who quietly listened while he poured out his long list of problems. Then the friend began to talk about the success power of the name *Jesus Christ*.

The troubled businessman said: "That's it. That is the answer. For many years I meditated nightly on the name and presence of Jesus Christ. I sent Him before me into my business day, and I did well. My marriage was peaceful and I had no health problems. It was when I stopped doing this that all these problems appeared."

Together they quietly meditated and declared that this man, his wife, and his business were all surrounded by the pure white light of the Christ, into which nothing negative could penetrate and out of which only good could come. They affirmed that Jesus Christ was taking control of his sales, his marriage, his health—guiding him every step of the way. Then they spoke the word releasing his life to the perfect outworking of the Christ presence.

With a sense of peace he had not known for months, he

went on his way. As he meditated nightly on these ideas, improvement came in all areas of his life: peace in his marriage, increased health, and success in his sales work.

A troubled businesswoman was distraught because her estranged husband had threatened to declare bankruptcy. If he did, it meant she would be left to face a number of their financial obligations alone.

As she talked with a friend, they agreed that there was colossal power for accomplishment in the name *Jesus Christ.* For a while they meditated together, surrounding her husband, their financial affairs and their lives with the Christ Presence. Then they declared that Jesus Christ was mightily at work, producing perfect results then and there.

Her husband changed his mind and decided to face up to his financial responsibilities, rather than declare bankruptcy. She obtained a better job, gained an inner tranquillity, and, when a divorce finally came, it was executed peacefully with a satisfactory settlement. This seemed a miracle, since previous indications had been that it would be a bitter, hard-fought experience.

HOW THE PROSPERING POWER OF THE CHRIST WORKED FOR THE AUTHOR

In 1961, great changes for good had come suddenly in my life, and I knew I would be moving to a new area to begin a new ministry. Since no funds were available for such a purpose, I was concerned about how I would be able to launch such an undertaking financially. The sudden change had caught me without personal funds for that purpose.

Meanwhile I was lecturing in Florida. A friend asked me to meet weekly with her for a time of meditation while I was there. In our weekly meditations, we called upon the name *Jesus Christ*. One night I said to her: "Let's pray about my new ministry. I don't know where to begin. I have no money with which to start this venture, and don't know of anyone who does."

As we sat quietly and affirmed that Jesus Christ was in charge of this new undertaking, was showing me what to do, and was opening the way financially, the name of one person who lived in the new area came to me. I did not know her personally, but had heard she was interested in Truth. I resolved then that after moving and getting settled, I would contact her.

When I phoned her, she was delighted to hear from me and insisted upon paying me a call. When she arrived, she handed me a check for several hundred dollars. She said: "Several years ago I conducted a Truth study group, and we accumulated a small amount of money. The group disbanded, but they asked me to place the money in savings, so that when someone appeared to start a new ministry, there would be something available to help out."

I had no way of knowing this. I only knew, through meditation, that I was supposed to contact her. Again, the prospering power in the name Jesus Christ had asserted itself!

Those few hundred dollars proved to be manna from heaven, which helped to launch that new ministry.

THE PROSPERING POWER OF THE LORD'S PRAYER

There is a tremendous prospering power in affirming the Lord's Prayer. (Matthew 6:9-13) Instead of taking it for granted and breezing through it in the usual fifteen seconds, begin to speak it over and over, slowly, deliberately, authoritatively, and you will feel its electrifying, energizing, transforming effect upon your life.

A troubled woman was in the process of getting a divorce. It left her feeling somewhat as major surgery does: terrible at first, but worth it, based on the knowledge that healing was in process. Hers had been a stormy, unhappy marriage of many years' standing which had only gotten worse, even after much prayer and inspirational study.

When the break came, she was suddenly left alone and without funds. A court order would eventually give her stipulated financial support, but such things take time. Meanwhile, she had her usual living expenses to meet.

Having read of the dynamic power of the Lord's Prayer, she decided to begin speaking it forth fifteen times a day. As she did, she gained great peace of mind and an inner assurance that she would be provided for. Through relatives, friends, part-time jobs, and the sale of cast-off household items she was financially provided for until financial support had been obtained for her through the courts.

As she continued daily in affirming the Lord's Prayer, a friend obtained a fine job for her, and she began building a "brave new world," accompanied by peace and pleasantness. She said later: "I will never again fear going without. I have the formula: daily affirmation of the Lord's Prayer."

Jesus was quite positive in all His affirmations. He made big claims on God, and demonstrated them. His prayers were filled with strong decrees. The Lord's Prayer is a series of determined affirmations.

In the American Standard Version of the Bible, the Lord's Prayer sounds like a petition, but in other versions, particularly the Fenton translation, the Lord's Prayer is a series of affirmations.

Paracelsus, a sixteenth-century physician in Zurich, spoke of how he caught flashes of genius through speaking, over and over, the Lord's Prayer.

Why is it so powerful? Perhaps because it tunes you in to

the same miracle consciousness that Jesus had for manifesting prosperity, when He multiplied the loaves and fishes to
feed thousands, paid taxes with money from the fish's
mouth, and turned water into the finest wine.

*Prayerfully repeating the Lord's Prayer is a great success formula
for invoking healing, peace of mind, vitality, right action in one's affairs, prosperity, and guidance, as well as a great power for breaking
up and dissolving hard conditions quickly.* As you use it daily,
this great prayer may even shock you into greater good than
you have ever known![3]

CASUAL AFFIRMATIONS WORK, TOO

Along with more formal methods of affirmation, the
casual spoken word that is positive and uplifting has great
power for producing like results. We see this success technique used in the affairs of many great men.

Winston Churchill planned and affirmed his way to success. Early in his career, he decided he wanted to go into
politics, but he was an unknown. He purposely got a news-
paper job that took him to the trouble spots of the world,
where he wrote vivid, on-the-spot accounts of what was
happening. In this way he became well known to many
readers back in England.

Later, he came home and ran for various political offices.
Each time he was defeated, he ran for another office. One
biographer has said that the most mystifying aspects of
those elections was Churchill's attitude when he lost. He
acted as though he had won!

After one election in which he had lost, Churchill turned

---

3. You will find an entire chapter on the Lord's Prayer in Catherine
Ponder's *The Millionaire from Nazareth* (Marina del Rey, CA: DeVorss &
Co., 1979), Chapter 5.

to the winner and said, ''I don't think the world has heard the last of either of us.'' This remark confused the winner so much that he rushed out to recheck the election returns, to make sure that *he* and not Churchill had really won.

Your casual, uplifting words can inspire others to tremendous success. We see this in the life of Franklin Roosevelt. A man named Louis Howe became convinced of Roosevelt's potential success twenty years ahead of time, and he even mapped out a timetable for FDR's future success.

They became close friends and co-workers, and Howe was addressing Roosevelt as ''Mr. President'' twenty years before his election to the presidency. When Roosevelt became ill, Louis Howe gave this illness no power, as he went on planning and affirming that Roosevelt would become President.

Twenty years later, when Roosevelt was elected, Howe celebrated by opening a bottle of sherry that he had bought years ahead of time and had saved for the occasion.

HOW CASUAL WORDS PROSPERED A JANITOR

A janitor's wife learned of the power of the casual word and put it to work constructively. Her husband had been working for the same business firm for fifteen years. They had informed him they were paying him top salary in his field, would pay no more, and that no other firm would pay more.

He had accepted this statement as true and was in a state of financial despair as living costs mounted.

His wife began to say: ''Honey, things are going to get better for us financially. Our income will increase.'' He only shook his head at these bold statements, but his wife persevered in her words.

One day he received a letter from the lieutenant governor of the state, saying they needed a man to head up the janitorial department at the state capitol, which was located in the town where this man lived. The letter stated that this man had been recommended for the job, and asked him, if interested, to apply.

In a few days he had been interviewed and hired at a beginning salary of $150 more per month than he had previously made. As a state employee he received graduated pay increases as well as vacation, retirement, and sick leave benefits—none of which he had had in his former job.

In his new job he was relieved of the backbreaking work he had done for years. He spent his time supervising other employees in the use of labor-saving cleaning equipment. One day the governor approached him in the capitol and thanked him for the good job he was doing in cleaning and beautifying the building. This janitor was surprised to learn that a member of the firm for which he had worked previously was often in the capitol on business, had learned of this job vacancy, and had quietly recommended him, feeling he deserved better employment.

His wife, a domestic worker, continued saying to her husband: "Things are getting better for us financially, and our income will continue to increase." Soon her longtime employer decided to double her salary! Not knowing of the power there is in casual words, her friends all shook their heads in amazement.

You can work miracles in your life, and in the lives of others, through your casual, uplifting, prosperous words. You can also work financial miracles by speaking forth prosperity affirmations for at least five minutes a day. These are ways of creating your prosperity mentally first.

SUMMARY

1. The third way to create your prosperity mentally is by speaking the word of prosperity.

2. The words *utter* and *outer* have similar roots. What you utter becomes outer in your world.

3. It has been estimated that the spoken word of prosperity can speed up results by as much as eighty percent.

4. Be definite in your words about prosperity, if you want prosperity to be definite about you.

5. For every fifteen minutes of inspirational study, you should spend five minutes speaking affirmations, if you want tangible prosperity in your life. Reading *about* prosperity isn't enough.

6. When you speak prosperity affirmations, a tremendous force is set up in the invisible that definitely affects substance, molding it into tangible results.

7. By using prosperity affirmations, you are not trying to make God give you anything. You are only opening your mind to receive the lavish abundance He has already provided for you.

8. There is prospering power in the Christ consciousness. By using "Jesus Christ" affirmations, and through constant affirmation of the Lord's Prayer, prospering power is released.

9. You can work financial miracles in your life by speaking forth prosperity affirmations for five minutes a day.

10. Your casual spoken words of prosperity and success have prospering power, too, for yourself and others.

THE SECRET OF
PERMANENT
PROSPERITY

— Chapter 6 —

By now, your "gold dust" formula for prosperity is becoming clear:

First, you cleanse your mind for prosperity.

Second, you create your prosperity, mentally, in writing, pictures, and words.

These are all ways of opening your mind to prosperity and *receiving it*.

But there is still another way to give your prosperity a permanent, enduring basis. This is the most fascinating and mystical prosperity law of all.

The ancients knew about it, and practiced it as "ten, the magic number of increase." They invoked the number of increase through systematic tithing or returning to their gods a tenth of their game, crops, and other channels of income.

The word *tithe* means "tenth." People of all great civilizations have felt that ten was the magic number of increase,
and have invoked it by tithing. These included the ancient
Egyptians, Babylonians, Persians, Arabians, Greeks, Ro-
mans, and Chinese.

In modern times, the magic number of increase still can
be invoked through the act of consistent tithing.

A housewife in Southern California learned she could
tithe her way to prosperity, and decided to try it. She and
her husband had seven growing children, for whom they
had struggled financially, even though her husband worked
for one of the major television studios.

After she began to tithe from their current income, an
opportunity opened for some of her children to appear in
television commercials. For this they were well paid. As
they tithed from this income, the way opened for all her
children to do television commercials, from which they
received handsome residuals.

They continued to tithe from all channels of income, and
within two years this family had moved into a large, beautiful home, the husband had received a better job, and all
the children were working in their spare time on television.
Trust funds were set up for the children's education, and
their futures were assured financially.

A friend said: "Doing television commercials is such
competitive work that I don't see how your children have
done so well. The average actor feels lucky to get two or
three jobs a year doing commercials, yet your children have
appeared in thirty this past year."

The mother explained: "Ten is the magic number of increase. We tithe all channels of income, so it isn't strange
that our children would receive ten times as much work as
those actors who don't tithe. It is the prosperity law."

TITHING, A MILLIONAIRE'S FORMULA

As the Bible's first millionaire, Abraham learned this success secret from the Babylonians, who were among the most prosperous people of the past. The Babylonians first advocated savings, home ownership, insurance, and other sound financial practices.

Abraham passed along the tithing law of prosperity to his grandson Jacob, who included it in his success covenant.[1]

God later gave Moses specific instructions about tithing for the Hebrews.[2] As long as the people of the Old Testament tithed, they prospered. But when they no longer put God first financially, during the reign of Solomon, the kingdom divided and the children of Israel went into Babylonian exile. When the "remnant" returned to Jerusalem, the prophet Malachi reminded them they must again tithe if they wished to prosper. He promised that the "windows of heaven" would open to them if they again invoked *ten*, the magic number of increase.

In the New Testament, both Jesus and Paul were tithers.[3] It was a required temple practice. As a Jew, Jesus paid tithes. A Pharisee in Jesus' time was required to spend a fourth of his income for religious giving. Paul was both a Pharisee and the son of a Pharisee. From his youth, he had been required to give a fourth of his income to God. *Tithing was a household word in Bible times.*

The ancients intuitively knew that giving, sharing, and

---

1. See the Ponder books *The Millionaires of Genesis*, Chapters 2, 3 and 6, and *The Prosperity Secret of the Ages*, Chapter 9.
2. See the Ponder books *The Millionaire Moses*, Chapter 7, and *The Millionaire Joshua*, Chapter 6.
3. See *The Millionaire from Nazareth*, Chapter 9.

putting God first financially was the first step to permanent, enduring prosperity.

YOU CAN TITHE YOUR WAY OUT OF INDEBTEDNESS

The act of tithing, or giving back to God's work a tenth of one's gross income, is not something that some minister dreamed up as a means of raising money! It is a universal prosperity law, practiced throughout the centuries as a method of prospering people on a permanent basis.

When you give consistently to God's work, you open the way to receive consistently in your own.

Many people have a psychological block against tithing, because so many theologians have stressed what tithing would do for the church rather than what it could do for the individual. When you look up the great tithing promises in the Bible, such as that given by Malachi, you find that the Bible says that the individual who tithes will be prospered. It goes without saying that his church will be, too. But that is secondary, and not the primary cause for tithing. As L. E. Meyer wrote, "As you tithe, so you prosper."[4]

WHEN YOU CANNOT AFFORD TO TITHE

Perhaps you are thinking, "But I cannot afford to tithe." Then you cannot afford *not* to tithe!

The greater the present financial necessity, the greater the need for immediately invoking "ten, the magic number of increase."

---

4. The booklet *As You Tithe, So You Prosper* is available, free of charge, from Unity School of Christianity, Unity Village, MO 64065.

A businesswoman was in a financial bind. She had moved from one part of the country to another, and had gone into a new line of work. It was paying off, but not fast enough to meet her many expenses. She practiced all the laws of prosperity in an effort to demonstrate immediate cash. Nothing happened—until she remembered she had gotten careless about her tithing.

She sat down and wrote out a tithe check for fifty dollars, and mailed it. The next day she got additional calls for work that tided her over a period of financial strain. But nothing happened until she first tithed.

Many years ago I began tithing—at a time when I felt I could not afford to tithe, yet could not afford *not* to—since my financial needs were so great. I decided to test "ten, the magic number of increase," after reading the following account of how someone even more destitute than I had been prospered through tithing:

A man who was ten thousand dollars in debt, with his credit gone and a wife and four children to provide for, took a job as a day laborer in a mill, and with his family was compelled to live in a tent. He met two divinity students who convinced him that if he wanted to prosper again, he should tithe.

The same week he began tithing, the company offered him one of its houses in which to live. Within a year he was promoted to foreman. Ten years later he was free from debt, the owner of a flourishing lumber company, a luxury car, an airplane, and other things on a similar scale. He attributes his success to first recognizing his debt to God and then faithfully tithing his income.

I decided to try this prosperity formula of tithing, and it worked for me, also.

TITHING YOUR TIME ISN'T ENOUGH

A woman said: "I don't see why I should tithe my money. I tithe my time to God's work. I am a Sunday-school teacher."

I replied: "That's fine, but what are you trying to demonstrate? More time or more money?"

"Oh, I'd like to have more time, but I really need more money."

I suggested that she check out the tithing promises in the Bible. They all spoke of tithing money and financial assets. Nowhere does the Bible talk about tithing one's time—commendable though that is.

A woman in Florida learned about tithing, and began to tithe from her small retirement income. Immediately she was offered part-time work and accepted it, tithing from it. Then she realized that the Bible spoke of tithing a "tenth of everything." She had a savings account with five thousand dollars in it, and decided that she should tithe from that as well.

She then drew five hundred dollars out of her savings account, and gave it to the church where she had learned about the great law of tithing. Soon she heard from the local Social Security Board, asking that she come in and see them.

Her first reaction was one of fear: "Now what have I done wrong?" But upon visiting them she had a pleasant surprise. Rather apologetically, they said "We owe you some money. Because of a new government regulation, the fact that you were born before a certain date means that we owe you $1,250."

She said, "I'm getting a Social Security check every month, thank you."

"Yes, we know that, and you will continue doing so. Nevertheless, we owe you this additional sum."

After the necessary paper work was completed, she received a check!

Another tither wondered why her savings account did not seem to grow. First she would put money in it, and then take money from it. Finally it dawned on her that she was not tithing from the interest on that account.

As she began tithing on interest income, her savings began to grow steadily.

Similarly, another tither worried because his investments did not seem to prosper him as they should, until he realized he was tithing from other channels of income but had never tithed from his stocks. After tithing from his stock income, he felt guided to sell certain of his stocks and invest in others, which brought him a far more handsome income.

This man no longer worries about the ups and downs of the stock market, but feels that, with God as his financial partner, he will continue to be guided about his income from this channel. He continues to prosper.

WITHHOLDING THE TITHE BRINGS LACK

Robert LeTourneau, the engineering genius, became famous for his tithing. In his book, *Mover of Men and Mountains*,[5] he speaks of the time after he started tithing when business was so good that one year he decided to hold on to his tithe:

"God, we have had a good year. Instead of giving You Your tithe of $100,000, which the business owes You this year, I am going to reinvest that $100,000 in the business, and You will get that tithe and much more next year."

He suffered one financial reverse after another. Bad

---

5. R. G. LeTourneau, *Mover of Men and Mountains* (Englewood Cliffs, NJ: Prentice-Hall, 1960).

weather kept his construction work from going forward. At the end of the year, he was $100,000 in debt. He learned from that experience never to withhold the tithe, and never to try to bargain with God about it.

In reflecting upon the lesson he learned, he quipped, "It is all right to give God credit, but He can also use cash."

Later LeTourneau's tithes ran into the millions, and he had to form a private foundation just to handle the distribution of them.

A salesman had prospered so much through tithing that he was trying to convince the owner of his company to tithe from company income. He wanted to know what to say to the boss.

A friend suggested he remind his boss that many of this country's millionaires attribute their wealth to tithing: the Rockefellers, the Heinz people, the Quaker Oats people, the Kraft people.

Tithing is a tried and true method in business.

WHERE YOU GIVE IS IMPORTANT

It is important that you give where you are receiving spiritual help and inspiration.

A woman once said: "I have some apartments that I cannot keep rented, although I use all the prosperity laws. And don't tell me to tithe, because I'm already doing that."

Where are you tithing?"

"I can't see that it is important where I tithe, so I give my tithe to the church I used to attend. But I now attend where I get far more inspiration."

The answer was: "Tithe where you are getting your help and inspiration if you wish to be prospered. It is inconsistent to do otherwise. To get spiritual help from one place and tithe to another is like going to one doctor for help and trying to pay another; or like eating in one restaurant, yet paying for your meal in another. Giving where you are receiving spiritual help and inspiration keeps you in touch with the flow of supply."

TITHING HEALS

A woman started tithing for financial reasons and was prospered, but she had a surprise. For years she had tried to lose weight and had been unable to do so. Yet when she started tithing, she "tithed away fifteen pounds!"

Tithing helps free you from the negative experiences of life. A woman who is now in the millionaire bracket said: "When something negative happens to me, I know I have not given enough. A negative experience is always an indication to me to give. I ask, 'Father, what do I need to give?'"

There is one basic problem in life: *congestion.* There is one solution: *circulation.*

If your financial affairs have stagnated into indebtedness, hard times, and constant problems, you can clear up the congestion through beginning to trust God to help you through your act of tithing to Him. *Tithing is an act of faith that brings about circulation and dissolves congestion.*

A man in New York City wrote, "My first tithe took away a strange circulatory ailment which defied medical help."

Then he made a confession: "It took me three years to change my thinking so that I was able to tithe. I had always skipped the chapters on tithing in your books. Now I am dumbfounded by the immediate disappearance of that constant, dreadful pain in my right leg and foot, thanks to giving the first tithe of my life."

A man in the real-estate business in Southern California

got careless in the distribution of his tithes, and learned quite a lesson.

One month he gave his tithe to a problem-prone relative, rather than giving it to his church. Everything went wrong. His bank account got mixed up, and a number of checks bounced. A real-estate deal, from which he expected a commission of several thousand dollars, did not go through. Other channels of supply simply dried up, and he was left in a financial bind.

Everything stagnated until he again put God—and not a problem-prone relative—first financially.

There is nothing wrong in giving to one in need, if you are careful what you give. But by giving only money, you offer only temporary help and therefore keep him in poverty. It is far wiser to give him literature on how to use the laws of prosperity for himself. This will prosper him permanently, and make him independent of poverty programs or handouts. "Give a man a fish and you feed him for a day. Teach him *how* to fish and you feed him for a lifetime."

The ancient laws on tithing were very definite about where the tithe was to be given. The first tenth went to the priests and place of worship. This tithe was given impersonally. The giver had no say about how it was to be spent.

The second tithe was a festival tithe; the third, a charity tithe.

If you are giving several tenths of your income rather than only one tenth, then you may feel freer with your second and third tithe. But your first tithe should be given impersonally to God's work, with no stipulation as to how it is to be spent by the recipient.

WHERE YOU GIVE YOUR MONEY IS WHERE YOU GIVE YOUR FAITH

A woman who had long been in ill health gave her money generously to several medical funds, yet could not understand why the prayers of her minister and prayer group had not healed her.

She had not identified financially with her church and its prayers for her. She had identified financially with heart trouble, cancer, polio, and many of the world's ills, through her giving. That was where she gave her money, and that was where her faith was.

She needed to go all the way with God in her giving, if she wanted God to go all the way in healing her.

There are plenty of people in the world today who have no spiritual faith or religious affiliation, yet want to give. Perhaps it is a step forward for them to support medical funds as well as educational, cultural, civic and community projects. They need to be giving and that is the level of their understanding, so that is the level of their giving.

But the sooner you evolve out of that level to a more expanded level of giving, to those people and organizations that inspire and uplift mankind spiritually, the sooner you will help mankind find the Truth that heals and prospers. If the Truth movement were properly supported, its teaching would reach millions, through the mass media, and wipe out disease and poverty.

Emmet Fox put it succinctly: ''The Truth movement is the only thing that can save the world from its ills. Everything else has already been tried.''

The Internal Revenue Service allows you to tithe up to half of your adjusted income. A lawyer who tithes a tenth of his legal income, before expenses, has said: ''If I don't give it to God's work, I've got to give it in taxes. Since I do not get to keep it, I prefer to give it where it will help and spiritually inspire many people."

This man has prospered incredibly.

GROSS OR NET?

Sometimes people ask: "Should I tithe gross or net?"

A friend said: "I tried tithing net (after taxes), but found I never had money enough to pay my taxes. When I went all the way with God, and tithed gross (before taxes), there was *always* money to pay my taxes. Tithing gross took the strain off my financial affairs all the way around."

If you are not free to tithe from all channels of income, start tithing from one channel. If you do not feel guided to tithe gross, begin tithing net. The important thing is to begin invoking "ten, the magic number of increase," in some way. Expanded results will justify expanded giving.

History shows that the ancient Egyptians gave twenty percent, or two tithes, to their temples. The Hebrews gave four tithes, even after they were required to pay taxes to the Roman government, in New Testament times. The Hindus required their people to give a tenth unless they were poor. They required the poor to tithe two tenths, because they felt the poor needed to give more in order to expand their prosperity consciousness.

WHAT THE AUTHOR LEARNED FROM WITHHOLDING A TITHE

I once had a large tithe offering I had not released. Someone telephoned to say she was sending me a valuable gift. It was something I had wanted for a long time. But weeks, then months, passed, and I did not receive that gift.

Finally I asked for guidance as to why the gift had not arrived, and the thought came: "You have not given that tithe offering yet. You've got to give to make room to receive. Release that tithe. Turn it loose quickly and completely."

I did. On that same day, in a distant city, my long promised gift was put in the mail to me, with this note:

"The strangest thing happened. After I telephoned you that I was sending your gift, it disappeared. For weeks I looked for it and could not find it. Finally, just this morning, it reappeared, and I am quickly sending it on to you as promised. I apologize for the delay."

That was a tremendous prosperity lesson to me. *When you do not give, you do not receive.* When you withhold the tithe, your good may even get lost. Giving is the first step in receiving.

WHEN SOMETHING IS TAKEN FROM YOU

Furthermore, *when you do not give voluntarily to the constructive experiences of life, you will have to give involuntarily to the destructive experiences of life. But give you must. It is the law of the universe.*

Sometimes that law works rather quickly. A woman once said, "I don't attend your lectures anymore, because the last time I did, as I was leaving the building afterward, someone snatched my purse."

It was interesting that, of all the people in attendance, this woman's purse was the only one that was taken. She had always said to the ushers at offering time: "I don't have an offering. I forgot my wallet."

In turn, she experienced a quick working of the law. She also proved that if you try to get something for nothing, something is taken from you. *Something for nothing is still nothing!*

When something is taken from you, it is an indication that you have not given—or have not given enough.

One woman said: "I cannot understand it. I've been greatly prospered through my study of the prosperity laws, even to the point of independent wealth—but I cannot keep it. People keep robbing me of my money. I make them loans of money as a means of helping them, but they never pay me back. I could take them to court and collect, but I want to get my money peacefully."

The reply was: "You say you have used all the prosperity laws. That means you tithe."

"Oh, no! How can I tithe, with all these people robbing me?"

It was suggested that she study the third chapter of Malachi, which plainly points out that *when you rob God, man robs you.* When you stop robbing God and begin putting Him first financially, then other people will stop robbing you. She had reversed the law, and she was getting a reversed result.

A millionaire businessman did not believe this. He had made his fortune the hard way, through his own blood, sweat, and tears, as well as through that of others. He refused to pay his employees well. He paid all his help the lowest possible price. He bought everything at a bargain, and for many years he seemed to get by with it.

Then one day it boomeranged on him in a way he would not have believed. His most prized "possession" was his beautiful wife. Suddenly another man appeared on the scene and took her from him.

He had unwittingly fulfilled the words of Malachi: "You are cursed with a curse, for you rob me." (Malachi 3:9)

TITHING BRINGS GOOD IN ALL
PHASES OF YOUR LIFE

A businessman in Detroit began tithing, and had a surprise. He was immediately relieved of his job of long standing. This was a job he never had liked.

The man then tithed from his unemployment check, and went on to a $20,000-a-year job, from which he continues to tithe.

At the time he tithed from his employment checks, he also was enduring an unhappy marriage. That dissolved.

He found that putting God first financially, through tithing, straightened out every phase of his life. He explained to a friend, "When I began tithing, limitation turned me loose."

Money invested in spiritual things is never lost; rather, it is multiplied many times over.

A SPECIAL NOTE FROM THE AUTHOR

Through the generous outpouring of their tithes over the years, the readers of my books have helped me to financially establish three new churches—the most recent being a global ministry, the nondenominational *Unity Church Worldwide*, with headquarters in Palm Desert, California. Many thanks for your help in the past, and for all that you continue to share.

You are also invited to share your tithes with the churches of your choice—especially those which teach the truths stressed in this book. Such churches would include the metaphysical churches of Unity, Religious Science, Divine Science, Science of Mind, and other related churches, many of which are members of The International New

Thought Movement. (For a list of such churches write The International New Thought Alliance, 7314 E. Stetson Drive, Scottsdale, Arizona 85251.) Your support of such churches can help spread the prosperous Truth that mankind is now seeking in this New Age of metaphysical enlightenment.

SUMMARY

The secret of permanent prosperity includes:

1. Using the number *ten* as the magic number of increase. The word *ten* means "tithe."

2. From primitive times, people of all great civilizations have practiced tithing as the universal law of prosperity.

3. Systematic giving opens the way to systematic receiving.

4. Tithing, giving, and sharing are always the first steps to permanent, enduring financial increase.

5. Many of our modern millionaires have proved it. Abraham, the Bible's first millionaire, tithed. As long as the people of the Old Testament tithed, they prospered. It was when they no longer put God first financially that their nation divided and they went into exile. When the "remnant" returned from exile, the prophet Malachi reminded them they must again tithe if they wished to prosper. Both Jesus and Paul were tithers; it was a required temple practice in their time.

6. The greater the present financial need, the greater the need to tithe.

7. Tithing your time isn't enough. The Bible promises prosperity to those who tithe a tenth of *all* channels of income. This includes tithing from savings accounts, stocks, real estate, inheritance, salary and bonuses.

8. Tithing heals, because it is an act of faith that brings about circulation and dissolves congestion.

9. Where you give is important. Tithe a tenth of your gross income at the point or points where you are receiving spiritual help and inspiration. Give it impersonally, with no strings attached. Giving to needy relatives or in other personal ways is not tithing.

10. When you do not give voluntarily to the constructive experiences of life, you will have to give involuntarily to the destructive experiences of life. Give you must. It is the law of the universe.

PART II:

OTHER WAYS TO
DEMONSTRATE
PROSPERITY

PROSPERITY THROUGH
THE DIVINE PLAN

— Chapter 7 —

People have sometimes said: "Your basic formula for demonstrating prosperity (as given in the first six chapters of this book) is great for people who know what they want out of life. But I don't know what I want, so how can I demonstrate it?"

There is a special way you can manifest your heritage of unlimited good: by calling the divine plan of your life into expression. *The great truth is that there* is *a divine plan for your life, and that divine plan is the sublime plan. It includes health, happiness, abundance, and perfect self-expression.*

As you begin to dwell upon the divine plan, you will attract to yourself the ideas, opportunities, events, and people that are meant to be part of your life.

You do not have to try to figure out what the ideas, opportunities, or events are to be. Instead, you simply dwell on your divine plan and let it unfold people, places, and things to you.

This is the easy way to pray and demonstrate your good. This is the easy way to straighten out events and situations in your own life, as well as to pray for other people.

Simply affirm that the divine plan is coming forth in any given situation, knowing it will be the sublime plan and will include the greatest good of all concerned. The results will usually amaze you.

Charles Fillmore explained why in his book *Prosperity*:[1] "It is the divine plan that all expression or demonstration shall come through this gateway of man's mind."

I know a man who was suffering the agony of an unhappy marriage and divorce problems, indebtedness, confusion, and a limited income; but who went from that to a brand new job, filled with self-expression, at double his previous income, a happy new marriage, peace of mind, increased health, and a whole new lease on life—after he began affirming the divine plan at an apparently hopeless period in his life. This transformation came within just six months! Some of the prayer statements he used daily which helped bring about these results were these:

"I NOW RELEASE EVERYTHING AND EVERYBODY THAT ARE NO LONGER PART OF THE DIVINE PLAN OF MY LIFE. EVERYTHING AND EVERYBODY THAT ARE NO LONGER PART OF THE DIVINE PLAN OF MY LIFE NOW RELEASE ME."

"I NOW LET GO AND LET GOD UNFOLD THE DIVINE PLAN OF MY LIFE. I AM NOW ATTUNED TO THE DIVINE PLAN OF MY LIFE. I NOW COOPERATE WITH THE DIVINE PLAN OF MY LIFE. CHRIST IN ME NOW MANIFESTS THE DIVINE PLAN OF MY LIFE QUICKLY AND IN PEACE."

_____

1. Unity Books, Unity Village, MO 64065, 1936.

"I NOW RECOGNIZE, ACCEPT, AND FOLLOW THE DIVINE PLAN OF MY LIFE AS IT IS REVEALED TO ME, STEP BY STEP. I REJOICE IN THE DIVINE PLAN, WHICH IS THE SUBLIME PLAN, AND WHICH INCLUDES HEALTH, WEALTH, HAPPINESS, AND PERFECT SELF-EXPRESSION FOR ME NOW."

THE EASY WAY TO UNFOLD YOUR GOOD

I first read the phrase "divine plan" in Florence Shinn's book *The Game of Life and How to Play It*.[2] She was an artist, from a prominent Philadelphia family, who became a metaphysician in New York City many years ago. Mrs. Shinn believed that the spoken word of Truth released the answer to every problem, and she had an affirmation to use for every situation. Proof that she was successful in helping people is shown in the popularity of her books, which contain many accounts of the affirmations given and the results obtained by those who sought her help.

There are many people in the world today who do not know what they want to do with their lives. If they would daily declare the divine plan for themselves, they would not have had to know specifically. They would unfold into it naturally.

Each of us comes forth on this earth plane with the divine plan for our life wrapped up within our soul nature. This divine plan longs to manifest for us. Calling on it releases it.

It matters not what age you are, how long you have lived, what you have done or have not done with your life. If you will begin daily to declare the divine plan for your life, it will lead you to your good.

---

2. Florence Shinn, *The Game of Life and How to Play It*, (Marina del Rey, CA: DeVorss & Co., 1978; originally published in 1925).

THE AUTHOR'S CHILDHOOD SENSE
OF A DIVINE PLAN

If parents would affirm the divine plan for their children when they are small, or even prenatally, there would be no confusion or uncertainty about the children's future. Each child would be intuitively guided into the divine plan of his life, and his parents would recognize that plan and be in agreement with it.

From my own childhood experience, I am convinced that there is a divine plan implanted in us prenatally. Even as a small girl I had a sense of destiny. I recall taking long walks in the woods, when the weeds were still higher than I was. In those quiet times I would often literally "ponder" my future.

I had a strong feeling, even then, that there was something "special" and "different" that I was supposed to do with my life. I intuitively knew even at that early age, that I was to serve humanity in some way. I often wondered if I was to do so as a teacher, nurse, or doctor. It was years later that my "special" calling became apparent —that of minister and writer in the metaphysical field. If I had known how to affirm the divine plan for my life at that early age (or if someone else had known how to do so for me), it may have accelerated my unfoldment into my life work considerably.

HOW A HOUSEWIFE MANIFESTED THE
DIVINE PLAN FOR HER LIFE

A certain housewife had always wanted a large family of children. But, after giving birth to her first child, her doctor informed her that her health would not allow her to have any more children.

When her daughter grew up, the mother became very restless and wanted to do something more with her life, but she did not know what. Then she learned that there is a divine plan for every person's life. In meditation, she prayed: "FATHER, IF YOU HAVE A DIVINE PLAN FOR MY LIFE, SHOW ME WHAT IT IS. HELP ME TO KNOW IT AND TO DO IT." After praying in this way, she relaxed and stopped straining for her good.

Soon the minister of her church called and asked her to work in the Sunday school. This request thrilled her, because she loved working with children. It was as though her desire for a large family was being satisfied.

She continued to affirm the divine plan for her life, and soon met an old college friend whose husband was a school principal. The friend asked, "Don't you have a degree in science?"

She did.

The friend said: "My husband is always looking for science teachers. Right now he is desperate for a physics teacher."

A few days later, this woman was hired as a substitute teacher in the school. She returned to college at night and during the summer, and took additional courses. She loved teaching. She loved children. *This* proved to be the divine plan for her life. She found that when she began to affirm the divine plan for her life, it took away the confusion, uncertainty, and sense of mistakes.

HOW TO CLEAR THE WRONG PEOPLE OUT OF YOUR LIFE

Many people are striving for things or situations in life which are not right for them. Many are even striving for people who do not belong to them.

A woman asked a spiritual counselor to affirm that she

would marry a certain man. The counselor replied that she could not speak the word in this way, because that man might not be a part of the divine plan of the woman's life.

Instead, the counselor affirmed that the next step in her divine plan might manifest; that the people, places and things which were a part of this plan might manifest quickly and in peace; and that everything and everybody else might fade out of her life and find their good elsewhere.

Though the woman continued to see the man for a time socially, nothing happened. As she continued dwelling on the divine plan, she met another man who quickly fell in love with her. They were soon married.

This woman later realized that she had previously been striving for someone who was not right for her. *If you have to force someone or something into your life, that is not part of your good. What you fight to get, you must fight to keep.*

But when you affirm the divine plan, those people and situations that are not a part of it begin to move out of your life. As you continue affirming the divine plan, those people and situations that are a part of it find their way into your life easily and naturally, unattended by fuss or bother. This is the easy way to live life successfully.

A young woman had been in love with a man, but he had not proposed marriage to her, so friends persuaded her to transfer her affections to someone else. She practically promised to marry the second man, but against her better judgment.

When the man she really loved moved out of her life, she felt very concerned. She did not feel right about the second man, whom her friends favored.

One day she shared her concern with a friend who was a Truth student. The friend said: "The way to solve this dilemma is simply to affirm that the divine plan for your life is manifesting now, quickly and in peace. Then watch and see what happens."

As she began doing this, an interesting thing happened. The man whom her friends favored faded out of her life quickly, and the man she really loved reappeared and they were soon married. The flow of events convinced her friends they had been wrong in their choice.

Later she said to her friend: "I would have married the wrong man, had he not released me and left. But when he departed the right man reappeared again." The friend reminded her that affirming the divine plan had cleared out of her life the man who was not right for her, and had brought the right one back into her life at just the right time.

THE DIVINE PLAN OFTEN BRINGS CHANGES

There is nothing new about this idea. Plato knew there was a divine plan for man's life. He called it the "divine design" and said: "Everything changes according to a divine design. We live in transition."

The one thing you must be prepared for, when you start calling on the divine plan, is transition and change. Nearly every one of us has wandered away from the divine plan of his life. When you begin to dwell upon the divine plan, you may find changes taking place in your life very quickly. Instead of resisting and resenting them, recognize them for what they are—part of your divine plan which can only lead you to expanded good if you will let it.

A businesswoman began affirming the divine plan of her life. So many changes came about so quickly, it was as though a cyclone had struck her affairs. But new and wonderful conditions took the place of the old, dissatisfying ones.

The prayer statement she used daily was: "I AM FULLY EQUIPPED FOR THE DIVINE PLAN OF MY LIFE. I AM MORE THAN

EQUAL TO THE SITUATION, AS I EXPAND QUICKLY INTO THAT
DIVINE PLAN.''

HOW TO FREE YOURSELF FROM AN OLD CYCLE

Most of us want freedom from something. Often we have
completed a cycle in our growth and progress, but we do
not know how to become free from that old cycle so as to
progress in new ways.

Usually we have learned what we can from a given set of
circumstances. We have given what we could to those circumstances. Yet we remain in them, not knowing how to
free ourselves. Speaking the word for the divine plan begins
to free us of worn-out circumstances, experiences, and relationships of the past or present.

From a business standpoint, instead of worrying about
your job, your business, or your firm, speak the word for its
divine plan to manifest. Affirm that the divine plan for that
business or organization may manifest quickly, and it will.

*Whenever you need guidance about people or events, declare that the
divine plan is manifesting in these situations or in the lives of those
people. You may be amazed at how quickly things will right themselves.*

A businessman found himself at the end of an old cycle,
but did not seem able to free himself from it. He had been
widowed for some time and wished to remarry, but felt it
would probably be necessary to get into a new environment
and set of circumstances before that would happen. He had
shared life with his wife in these present circumstances, and
he thought their mutual friends would resist the idea of his
marrying anyone else. He had gone as far as he could in his
present job, both financially and in the expression of his
talents. He had grown restless and needed new worlds to

conquer. But he seemed held by old memories, relationships, and circumstances, and did not know how to free himself from them.

One day he attended a class in metaphysical instruction for the first time. The teacher declared that there was a divine plan for each one in the class. She said that the divine plan was unfolding for each one and that each would recognize his divine plan as it began to work out.

Her positive words of assurance gave this man hope. He joined the others, at the end of each class period, when they affirmed together: "THERE IS A DIVINE PLAN FOR MY LIFE. THAT DIVINE PLAN IS UNFOLDING FOR ME NOW."

At first, nothing seemed to happen when he affirmed this, but he did begin to feel better and more hopeful. As he continued attending the class, he met a businessman from a nearby town and they became friends. They discovered that they wished to go into the same kind of business, but each needed a partner. Each felt that an old cycle of activity was over for him, and that he wanted to launch forth into new experiences. This man daily declared: "NOTHING CAN HINDER THE DIVINE PLAN OF MY LIFE. NO ONE CAN DELAY THE DIVINE PLAN OF MY LIFE. WHAT GOD HAS GIVEN ME CANNOT BE DIMINISHED."

In a matter of months, this previously unhappy man had concluded his old business affairs and moved to the nearby town, where he went into business with his new partner. Together they continued affirming the divine plan for their lives and for their new business.

Not only did their new business flourish, but within the year this previously lonely widower happily married a fine woman, who was also affirming the divine plan!

One business organization decided to test the prospering power of affirming the divine plan. Its board of trustees began affirming the divine plan at their business meetings.

They quickly observed a new surge of growth in business, which brought increased prosperity. New people appeared, who wanted to help carry the business forward into expansion. This happened as the trustees affirmed: "THROUGH THE DIVINE PLAN, THIS BUSINESS NOW MOVES FORWARD INTO ITS EXPANDED GOOD."

HOW TO PRAY SUCCESSFULLY FOR YOURSELF AND OTHERS

It is good to affirm for others: "I RELEASE YOU TO THE DIVINE PLAN OF YOUR LIFE. CHRIST IN YOU REVEALS TO YOU THE DIVINE PLAN. YOU UNFOLD INTO IT QUICKLY AND IN PEACE." So often we have mistakenly advised others of what we felt they should do, and have carried heavy emotional burdens as a result, when our only responsibility was to affirm the divine plan for them and let them unfold their good in their own way.

Declare often for yourself: "CHRIST IN ME NOW REVEALS, UNFOLDS, AND MANIFESTS THE DIVINE PLAN OF MY LIFE, QUICKLY AND IN PEACE."

One man's life was transformed after he prayed: "FATHER, IF YOU HAVE A DIVINE PLAN FOR MY PERSONAL LIFE, SHOW ME WHAT IT IS. DRAW TO ME THE PEOPLE WHO BELONG IN MY LIFE NOW, AND UNITE ME WITH THEM."

WHEN YOUR GOOD IS DELAYED

When you affirm the manifestation of the divine plan for your life, it may begin unfolding quickly. If so, you must be willing to let go of the old and quickly expand into your divine plan, accepting whatever changes are involved in people, environment, and events. As Emerson has stated, "For everything you gain, you lose something."

However, just the opposite may happen when you begin affirming the divine plan: changes may come slowly or not at all. If your good seems delayed, it may be a matter of "divine timing." Even though you feel ready for your new good, the new people and events that are to be connected with your divine plan may not yet have reached their point of fruition in your life. This is the time to declare that the divine plan of your life manifests under "divine timing." To human sense, that divine timing may seem slow, but when it begins manifesting your new good, it often happens so quickly as to be breathtaking. You must be ready for it when it comes.

Often the divine plan does not seem to work in our behalf until we have brought order into a present situation. As long as there is still something for us to do in a present situation, our new good cannot appear. A loving Father seems to withhold the next development until order is first established in the present situation and in the present state of mind. It is wise at such times to declare "divine completion" for the present situation, and then follow through in outer ways to bring that completion about. As you get things in order and bring them to a conclusion, this frees the next step in the divine plan to begin manifesting for you.

The world of nature knows about divine timing. At a recent world's fair, I saw a science film which described the life of certain plants that bloom in the desert. The film explained that these plants blossomed in that desert climate only when conditions were just right. The plants would often wait for years for the right conditions, before they blossomed.

Like the plant in the desert, awaiting the right conditions in which to blossom, we sometimes have to await just the right time in our soul growth to enjoy our expanded good. Meanwhile, by meeting our present circumstances non-resistantly, we may be developing certain soul qualities and talents which will prepare us for that time.

During such periods, no matter how much we persist in dwelling on increased health, wealth, or happiness, our good may not appear, because we are not yet ready to receive it and maintain it. If we receive it during such a period, it would be a premature, forced growth, and would not last. Under such circumstances, we may find our good coming more slowly under divine timing. But later we will realize that it came at just the right time for our long-range benefit.

The author of the book of Ecclesiastes knew the importance of divine timing, and talked about it in that familiar passage: "For everything there is a season and a time for every matter under heaven. . . . He has made everything beautiful in its time." (Ecclesiastes 3:1, 11)

This wise man, often referred to as "the Preacher," knew about the divine plan. In that same passage he wrote, "That which is already has been; that which is to be, already has been." (Eccelsiastes 3:15)

If you are not sure what you want to do with your life, meditate daily on the following statements. Affirm them often, and you will soon begin to see the divine design unfolding.

"EVERY PLAN WHICH MY FATHER IN HEAVEN HAS NOT PLANNED FOR ME IS NOW DISSOLVED IN MY LIFE. THE NEXT STEP IN THE DIVINE PLAN QUICKLY MANIFESTS. THE DIVINE IDEA, THE DIVINE PLAN FOR ME, NOW COMES TO PASS. NEW DOORS OF GOOD NOW OPEN TO ME! WITH A CONFIDENT SPIRIT, I NOW GO FORTH INTO A LIFE OF HAPPINESS, SECURITY, AND ABUNDANT LIVING IN THE NAME OF JESUS CHRIST."

SUMMARY

1. If you do not know what you want to do with your life, begin calling the divine plan of your life into expression.

2. The divine plan is the sublime plan for your life. It includes health, happiness, abundance, and perfect self-expression.

3. As you begin to dwell on the divine plan, you will attract the ideas, opportunities, events, and people that are meant to be a part of your life.

4. Decree that you release everything and everybody that are no longer part of the divine plan of your life, and that everything and everybody that are no longer part of the divine plan now release you. This dissolves worn-out relationships and conditions, and frees you to your expanded good.

5. It matters not what age you are, how long you have lived, or what you have or haven't done with your life. Affirming the divine plan can still lead you into that which is best for you.

6. Affirming the divine plan takes away all sense of confusion, uncertainty, and mistakes.

7. When we affirm the divine plan for children, they are intuitively guided into it.

8. When you begin calling on the divine plan, prepare yourself for the possibility of change. Nearly everyone has wandered away from the divine plan of his life, and changes often come quickly when he begins thinking in this new way.

9. Recognizing the divine plan can cause organizations as well as individuals to prosper. Instead of outlining what you think is best for others, the wise way to think of them and pray for them is by declaring that their divine

plan manifests quickly and in peace. Then what you had in mind for them, or something better, will manifest.

10. If your new good does not manifest quickly through calling on the divine plan, then you can know it is coming about under divine timing. The new people and events that are to be connected with your divine plan have not yet reached the point of fruition in your life. Get things in divine order. Then relax by declaring that your divine plan will manifest for you under divine timing.

PROSPERITY THROUGH THE WISDOM CONCEPT

— Chapter 8 —

Solomon demonstrated prosperity through using the wisdom concept. We can, too.

The word "wisdom" means knowledge. True wisdom is knowledge from within. It is an inner knowing. This is the kind of wisdom Solomon developed, and which made him a multimillionaire.

As he turned within and asked for guidance, he intuitively knew what to do about every situation that was presented to him. He became so clairvoyant about people and situations that he could "see through them." They could not fool him.

Through listening to that inner knowing, he prospered mightily. As you read the book of Proverbs, you discover that he often affirmed riches for himself through the wisdom concept. In one of his most famous passages he affirmed: "I have counsel and sound wisdom." Then he affirmed what that inner knowing would do for him: "Riches and honor are with me, enduring wealth and prosperity." (Proverbs 8:14–18) These affirmations contain prospering power for us as we use them, too.

In this enlightened age, we are learning to do as Solomon did: to turn within, ask for guidance, and follow through on that inner knowing that wells up from within us. This is wisdom that can prosper us mightily.

Several decades ago, I often would sit with a friend in daily periods of affirmation and meditation. Such an abundance of ideas for articles and books "welled up" within my thoughts during those periods, that I have been busy trying to get them all into print ever since.

TRUE EDUCATION WELLS UP FROM WITHIN

We are hearing much these days about the importance of education. The word "educate" means to lead out or draw out from within. One New Thought writer has predicted that the new education will "well up from within." This is the kind of education system that has prospering power and can lead a person to true success.

The people of the East have long known that true wisdom lies within the individual, and that it wells up from within *when given an opportunity to do so.* They have practiced prayer and meditation, as methods for contacting this wisdom within them, for centuries. Their meditation practices have now come to the attention of the Western world, and in the last few years increasing numbers of people have become fascinated with the power and practice of meditation.

Years ago it was reported that more than twenty-five thousand college students were meditating every day. That figure would doubtless be much higher today. Obviously

the prediction that New Thought writer made decades ago
is now coming true. Those in the field of education are
realizing that true education "wells up from within," and
they are encouraging the ancient method of attaining wisdom through meditation.

HOW THE WISDOM CONCEPT PROSPERS

Perhaps you are thinking: "But I need prosperity and
success now. I do not have much time for the practice of
meditation, nor can I wait years to perfect that method of
getting wisdom in order to be prospered. Surely there must
be a shortcut."

In a sense there is: by using the wisdom concept. Like
Solomon of old, many a successful person has used this
method and has become exceedingly prosperous.

Since the word "wisdom" means knowledge from within, and the word "concept" means a thought, idea, or notion, you can begin practicing the wisdom concept by dwelling upon the thought, idea, or notion of an indwelling
intelligence. This is simple to do, though its results are often
profound.

You can begin using the wisdom concept and reap its
benefits by realizing that all around you and within you
there is a Power which you can begin to tap at any time,
from which will flow ideas and energy that can transform
your life. *This Power comes alive within and around you as
unlimited wisdom and guidance, by your simply paying attention to
it, recognizing its presence, and asking its help.* It's as simple as
that.

The important thing is to realize the ever-present existence of this Power and ask its help often. The difference
between many a $12,000-a-year man and a $50,000-a-year

man is that the latter knows about this Power, has asked its help, and has gotten it, whereas the former has not.

When the world-renowned Einstein was asked the secret of his success he replied, "It is the result of intuition, an inner knowing."

REALTOR BECOMES MILLIONAIRE THROUGH WISDOM CONCEPT

A man in the real estate business told me how learning about the wisdom concept transformed his life. He had worked very hard, for very little, until he learned of this universal Power and its prospering power. He began spending a few minutes, early every morning, deliberately inviting this universal wisdom to give him guidance about his real estate transactions. Again and again, ideas began to flow to him from within about what to do and what not to do.

Soon after beginning this daily practice, he felt guided to buy a certain piece of property for twenty thousand dollars —and did so. Because of an inner urge to keep this property as an investment rather than resell it, he did just that. A few years later, he sold this same piece of property for a quarter of a million dollars! This property now houses a multimillion-dollar shopping center.

In describing the prospering power of the wisdom concept, this man said to me: "I am a Truth student of long standing. I have become a millionaire through turning within every morning, asking for guidance about my financial affairs, and then following through on the ideas and opportunities that came, regardless of what other people thought I should or shouldn't do. I am convinced that true wisdom comes from within, and contains the greatest prospering power there is.''

HOW DENTIST PROSPERS THROUGH
WISDOM CONCEPT

True wisdom reorients the individual from within. True
wisdom first expands one's mind and then it expands one's
world, as the individual listens to its guidance.

Another Truth student was a young dentist who learned
of the prospering power of the wisdom concept. Early in his
practice, he struggled to survive professionally and financially. Then through his study of Truth, he learned of this
universal power within and around him which would respond to his thinking about it and asking its help. This he
began to do daily, in early morning times of quietness. Also
he often silently asked its help as he went about his day.

He asked that divine wisdom show him how to expand
his dental practice so that he could help more people. The
affirmation he used was: "WITHIN ME IS THE WISDOM OF
THE AGES. THAT WISDOM NOW SHOWS ME HOW TO EXPAND MY
PRACTICE AND MY WORLD. THAT WISDOM NOW SHOWS ME
HOW TO PROSPER AS I HELP OTHERS.''

Soon after he began deliberately and directly asking for
help, a business associate suggested that this dentist install
six chairs in his office, rather than only the two, and that he
invite several young dentists to come to work for him on a
percentage basis, allowing them to use his equipment.

He did so, and this made it possible for these young doctors to get into practice immediately, without the usual
financial strain attending one just starting out. It also made
it possible for this young dentist to share in their income

and practice. The method worked very well, as all involved became prosperous and successful—thanks to the wise guidance that came to this man through a friend, after he asked divine wisdom to show him what to do.

DRESS DESIGNER GOES FROM POVERTY TO AFFLUENCE

There once was a woman who became a noted dress designer, but who, a few years previously, had been living in poverty, struggling to support herself and an elderly parent.

Then she learned of this universal wisdom that was within and around her. She began to set aside a certain time, every day, during which she got quiet and invited this power to give her guidance about her life. She said that when she first began this practice, nothing much happened. She would find herself thinking about her debts and all her troubles.

But as she daily practiced getting quiet anyway, it got easier. First she began to feel more peaceful, as the worry and fear subsided. Next she began to gain a sense of power and dominion over her thoughts, her feelings, and her world. This led her to realize that she *could* cope with her problems.

Then, in one of these quiet times, she began to think strongly about a certain business acquaintance whom she contacted. He offered her a job as a dress designer!

She knew very little about dress designing but she accepted the job anyway, feeling that divine wisdom would show her how to handle it. Daily, in her quiet times, she would ask divine wisdom to reveal to her all that she needed to know about designing dresses. Knowledge and ideas flowed to her. As those original ideas came, she acted upon them, and her career was assured. This woman went from poverty to soul-satisfying affluence, simply by asking divine wisdom to show her what to do.

HOW A MAN PROSPERED FROM USING SCRAP TIN

So often greater good has not come into our lives because we have not asked for it! We have not asked to be shown how to claim it.

Wisdom expands the mind. When you ask divine wisdom to reveal greater good to you, it does so by first expanding your mind, and then your world, through the ideas it gives you.

It was the multi-faceted genius, Walter Russell, who had no formal schooling, who once said: "I have faith that anything can come to one who trusts to the unlimited help of universal wisdom."

A man who heard about the prospering power of the wisdom concept decided to prove it first in a small way. In conversation with a friend, he said he believed divine wisdom could show him what to do about any problem. The friend challenged him by saying: "There is a pile of scrap tin which is about to go into the garbage can. It looks useless to me. Why don't you ask divine wisdom to show you what you can do with it?"

He accepted the challenge. Presently, there came into his mind the picture of a little matchbox. He began to cut and bend the tin, and had soon shaped a matchbox from it. Calling to him a small boy who was passing by, he asked the boy if he would like to sell the matchbox for twenty-five cents and receive a profit of ten cents from the sale. The boy was delighted and soon sold the matchbox. He then got busy selling others that the man made. Soon both man and boy had made a nice profit from that pile of tin which had seemed destined for the garbage can.

HOW THE WISDOM CONCEPT HEALS
AND PROSPERS AN ATTORNEY

Scientists tell us that we live in a sea of universal wisdom. This universal wisdom seems to be both immanent and transcendent—within and without. We can begin tapping this sea in far greater ways than ever before, just by recognizing its presence and asking its help. So often we have struggled alone unnecessarily, simply because we did not know about this power nor how to ask its help.

If you will begin spending just a short time every day thinking about this universal wisdom and asking its help about anything that concerns you, this practice will make every phase of your life more wonderful than it has ever been before!

A well-known lawyer was once asked how he had become famous for his brilliant work in court. He replied that he owed his success to contacting this great Universal Wisdom, in his quiet times of reflection and meditation.

This brilliant attorney said he not only got hunches of vital importance which enabled him to handle difficult court cases successfully, but that his health had been restored completely by an influx of power which had been contacted during meditation. He said he actually felt a universal energy flowing into him, restoring his health, at such times.

AFFIRMATIONS RELEASE WISDOM

In the third chapter of the book of Proverbs, Solomon promised that the man who dares to follow the inner leadings of divine wisdom will have a long life, riches, honor, pleasantness, peace of mind, health, and happiness.

We seem to contact this universal wisdom in several ways:

First, by recognizing its presence and asking for its help.

Second, by affirming that it is showing us what to do and is helping us do it. This seems to release the power from within us, as well as from within circumstances and people.

Psychologist William James knew about this universal wisdom. He considered it a deeper level of the mind. He taught that along with a conscious and subconscious mind, man also has a deeper level of mind—in which resides an infinite intelligence that longs to work for and through man. By recognizing it, giving it your attention, and decreeing it, you release this super-wisdom within.

If you will invite this infinite intelligence to solve any problem that concerns you, it will: "THERE IS AN ANSWER. DIVINE WISDOM NOW SHOWS ME THE PERFECT ANSWER. I RELAX, LET GO, AND LET IT INSTRUCT ME."

A schoolteacher decreed that divine intelligence was showing her what to write in a contest, so that she might win a trip to Europe. The ideas came in a rush, and she quickly submitted her entry—which won her the trip. Later, she could not remember what she had written—only that it came quickly after she had asked. Infinite intelligence is teeming with right answers and solutions, and awaits your attention. Your act of asking and affirming opens the channel for receiving that intelligence, as it did for this schoolteacher.

JOB TRANSFER COMES THROUGH THE
WISDOM CONCEPT

A government employee was advised by his doctor to move to the Midwest for his health. But when he applied for a transfer, he was informed that there were no openings and none anticipated. He and his wife even visited that area and personally talked to a number of people, in an effort to effect a transfer. Repeatedly they were told that nothing was available.

Then they attended a lecture and heard the wisdom concept explained. They began meditating daily, asking divine wisdom to show them what to do. Often they affirmed: "WE INVITE DIVINE WISDOM INTO EVERY PHASE OF OUR LIVES NOW. WE INVITE DIVINE WISDOM INTO THIS SITUATION NOW. DIVINE WISDOM IS OPENING WAYS WHERE, TO HUMAN SENSE, THERE IS NO WAY."

They felt so strongly the truth of these words that, after one meditation period, the wife started packing!

It worked. Soon the husband received word that a new government building was being built in one of the most beautiful cities in the Midwest, and that his application for a transfer was being honored. He was to report to work in just two weeks.

As his wife continued affirming that divine wisdom was at work in every phase of their lives, she was able to dispose of household effects quickly and to make the move on time. On her way out of town, she said jubilantly to a friend: "We had tried for two years to bring this about, but only met with obstacles—until we asked divine wisdom to help us. Then we got action quickly."

DIVINE WISDOM WORKS IN OTHERWISE
UNCONTROLLABLE SITUATIONS

When you find yourself in circumstances over which you seem to have no control, instead of fighting to survive in those circumstances, that is the time to call on divine wisdom. By calling on divine wisdom, you release it into the events which you seem unable to control.

A young housewife decided to entertain some of her husband's relatives at dinner. These particular relatives had criticized this young wife, saying that she was not a good cook or housekeeper but could only express along artistic lines. In order to show them how wrong they were, she resolved to prepare a good dinner for them and to serve it well. For the preparation she set aside a whole day.

When the day came, things started happening over which she seemed to have no control. Right after breakfast, a neighbor telephoned for help. She went over quickly, and found it necessary to remain with the sick neighbor until 11:30 a.m.

Returning home, she washed the breakfast dishes and was preparing a quick lunch for her husband, when he telephoned to say he was bringing a business associate home for lunch. It was then that she began calling on divine wisdom, to help her meet these unexpected events. Over and over she affirmed: "DIVINE WISDOM WORKS THROUGH ALL SITUATIONS FOR GOOD."

After a successful lunch, the postman brought a letter from a friend, saying she would be in town briefly between trains that afternoon and needed to see this woman, suggesting that they meet at the train station. When she prayed about whether to go to the train or not, she found herself affirming: "I TRUST DIVINE WISDOM IN THIS SITUATION. I TRUST

DIVINE WISDOM TO PRODUCE PERFECT RESULTS NOW.'' She felt guided to go, and did so—but the train was late.

After her friend arrived and they had chatted briefly, her visitor handed her a large package. Because of the time element, she then went straight home, rather than stopping to shop further for the dinner that night. On the way home she continued declaring to herself: ''DIVINE WISDOM HAS BEEN AT WORK IN THE SITUATION, PRODUCING PERFECT RESULTS QUICKLY.''

Upon opening the package at home, she found in it everything she needed for dinner that night: rolls, vegetables, eggs, a chicken—even a dessert. When dinner was served to her in-laws, they commented with surprise on what a fine cook she was.

This woman realized that in spite of such a hectic day, everything had worked together for good when she asked divine wisdom to help. She later learned that the man her husband had brought home so unexpectedly for lunch, had left his own home that morning vowing never to return. But in the delightful atmosphere he had found at her luncheon table, he changed his mind and returned to his family, vowing to do his part to make things more pleasant at home. The sick neighbor she had taken time to visit that morning, recovered and took up the study of Truth in earnest, realizing its power as a result of this woman's visit.

This woman found that divine wisdom has infinite ways of making things right, especially in situations that seem beyond our control.

SOLOMON'S COSTLY MISTAKE

This is perhaps the greatest thing we can learn about the wisdom concept: It works in and through everything and everybody in our lives for good, if we do not block it when things seem uncertain or even out of control.

You can save yourself considerable wear and tear when you learn simply to call on divine wisdom to help you meet life victoriously.

Solomon's impressive success came during the early years of his reign, when he made it a practice to ask divine wisdom for guidance about everything. As long as he followed that guidance he prospered, even to the point of becoming one of the richest men the world has ever known.

Later, when he was surrounded by vast wealth, Solomon forgot that his prosperity had come through the wisdom concept. He began to play politics, by seeking alliance with foreign powers who cared nothing about an infinite intelligence. Solomon began to seek their favor and guidance, rather than continuing to turn within for it. His multi-million-dollar empire was finally forced into exile and poverty.

From a study of Solomon's life, we observe both sides of the coin: prosperity, through following the inner leadings of divine wisdom; lack, through looking to people and events rather than to that indwelling wisdom.

THE WISDOM CONCEPT IS EASY TO USE

Developing the wisdom concept is easy, and its benefits are unlimited. For a few minutes every day, quietly invite this universal wisdom into your life. Ask its help about anything that concerns you. Then be quiet, receptive, open-minded. As you relax, not trying to force or compel them in any way, the thoughts and feelings that are for your highest good will begin to flow to you. The people and events that are for your highest good will find their way to you. As you continue daily to invite universal wisdom into your mind, body, financial affairs, and human relationships, remarkable things will happen. Affirm often: "I AM UNDER THE INFLUENCE OF DIVINE WISDOM."

Demonstrating prosperity through the wisdom concept is one of the surest ways.

SUMMARY

1. Solomon demonstrated prosperity through using the wisdom concept. You can, too.

2. True wisdom is knowledge from within. To educate means to draw out from within.

3. True wisdom lies within, and wells up within the individual when given an opportunity to do so.

4. Through the deliberate and daily practice of meditation, affirmation, quiet reflection, or spiritual study, you open the way for true wisdom to well up from within you. As you follow through on its ideas, you are led to the opportunities, events, or people that are a part of your prosperity.

5. The word "concept" means a thought, idea, or notion. You can also practice the wisdom concept by affirming that divine wisdom and intelligence are guiding you.

6. Practicing the wisdom concept not only prospers but also heals and harmonizes one's life.

7. We live in a sea of universal wisdom which is both immanent (within) and transcendent (without).

8. So often we have struggled unnecessarily because we did not know about this power within and around us, and did not ask for its help.

9. When you find yourself in circumstances over which you seem to have no (outer) control, do not fight them.

Call on divine wisdom to do its perfect work in the situation.

10. When you are up against a stone wall and do not know how to dissolve obstacles and barriers, call on divine wisdom to do its perfect work. The solution will come. Calling on divine wisdom is one of the surest ways to overcome all difficulties and demonstrate prosperity.

PROSPERITY THROUGH THE LOVE CONCEPT

— Chapter 9 —

To practice consistently the love concept is one of the quickest ways to overcome all your difficulties and demonstrate your spiritual heritage of unlimited good.

Since the word *concept* means "something conceived in the mind," the way to practice the love concept is to become filled with the idea of love inwardly, and then express it both inwardly and outwardly. This releases a high-powered energy that is instantly felt and responded to by people and situations.

World-renowned sociologists made experiments in the power of love at Harvard University several decades ago. They predicted that bombarding people and situations with thoughts of love could become a universal prescription for curing the world's ills.

There are those people who read self-help books and take numerous success courses, who get the idea that mind

144

power is all there is; that if they just use mind power suffi-
ciently, everything will come their way.

For a time they may seem right. They can produce
tremendous results through the power of thought and
through using its techniques, as described in some of the
foregoing chapters. The time usually comes, though, when
they realize that mind power is not enough, and they begin
to "spin their wheels" spiritually.

In your own life, you may go through periods when
Truth principles no longer seem to work for you suffici-
ently. If so, it may be that you need to use them more lovingly. The mind's eternal duty is to express in love. This is
the great lesson that mind has to learn, the lesson of love.
Mind power can become unbalanced when it is not used
lovingly.

*Practicing the love concept can do more to help you achieve your
goals than all the hard mental effort in the world.* If you get too
tense about what you want out of life and try to force it into
manifestation mentally, you can actually repel the very
good you are trying to manifest.

Use of the love concept magnetically draws your good to
you, in countless ways. This method takes the strain out of
demonstrating your good.

You can begin invoking the love concept by meditating
often upon the Biblical statement: "GOD IS LOVE." Dwelling
often on this statement keeps you from becoming too cold
or unloving. It can also cause a marvelous transformation
to take place in you and your world.

Invoking the love concept releases a certain kind of vibra-
tion that people appreciate and respond to. Dwelling on the
love concept makes you a magnet for your good.

Believing this, a businesswomen's group decided to
spend some time at their monthly meetings, for an entire
year, affirming love for the club and its members. This was

to be their experiment in proving the power of the love concept as a success principle.

Within a short time after the first meeting when they affirmed words of love, several of these middle-aged businesswomen got married! One career woman had been widowed for twenty-five years, but soon married happily and went off to southern California, to live with her husband in a beautiful new home he provided for her near the sea. So many women in that group got married during that year of affirming love that they had to reorganize the whole club!

The love concept works in both personal and impersonal ways. As we use it, it often brings new people and experiences into our life. It also releases more harmony and peace into our already established relationships.

LOVE CONCEPT DEVELOPS
A HARMONIOUS ATTITUDE

People sometimes hesitate to use the love concept because they think that to become filled with the thought of love is to become filled with a gushing kind of emotionalism. But love is sincere—often quiet. A gushing sort of emotionalism isn't true love, because it isn't sincere. Its expression doesn't fool anyone for long.

Famed psychologist Eric Fromm describes the love concept simply: "Love shows itself as a harmonious attitude toward life."

Psychologists state that one reason for mental illness, family problems, health problems, or financial failure is that many people do not have enough "give ability" toward life. They have a rigid set of rules about how life and people are supposed to be. When people and conditions do not measure up to their rigid rules, they criticize, condemn, find fault, resist, and resent. They are inharmonious, unloving, and unhappy. This leads to all kinds of problems, and they wonder why life never becomes what they want it to be.

Practicing the love concept helps us develop a noncritical attitude toward life and people. We become less rigid, less fixed, less resistant to life and people when they do not follow our personal set of rules. The love concept helps us to develop a more harmonious reaction than a negative one, even when life and people are not what we think they should be.

HOW THE LOVE CONCEPT HELPS NEIGHBORS

It is easy to have a harmonious reaction toward life and people when everything is going our way. If we can also remain harmonious, nonresistant, and uncritical when things go wrong, then we are practicing the love concept and giving it a chance to make things right, perhaps in ways we could not foresee.

A woman heard of the love concept and decided to use it for a troublesome neighbor, who often got very loud and disorderly. This neighbor would keep everyone in the neighborhood awake at night with his antics.

As the woman began daily to decree that divine love was at work in the situation, producing perfect results, the neighbor became peaceful. Soon there were no more outbursts.

Life is filled with opportunities for using the love concept and proving its harmonizing, adjusting, prospering power. We can begin testing it in the daily problems that confront us.

One reason the love concept is so powerful is because the word *love* produces a positive, harmonious, magnetic current when deliberately sent forth. This love current will break up opposing thoughts of hate and render them powerless. *The thought of inharmony can be dissolved, not only in the mind of the one practicing the love concept, but also in the mind of everyone with whom he comes in contact, so that countless people are harmonized and blessed by one person's practice of love.*

The average person is not aware that he possesses this mighty power to dissolve all negative emotions—his own and others. Nor is the average person aware that the word *love*, when persistently used, will transform conditions in mind and body, financial affairs, or interpersonal relationships.

When you find yourself tempted to resist, resent, or criticize people, situations, or life in general, that is the time to use the love concept. By holding to thoughts of love, you remain harmonious, as you bless the situation rather than add to the confusion.

HOW THE LOVE CONCEPT HEALS

Many persons, as a result of unhappy childhood experiences, have resistant places in their subconscious mental areas that do not readily yield to the power of thought or the spoken word. Yet words of love, repeatedly used, dissolve those resistant areas. Metaphysicians have known for years that the word *love* reconstructs, rebuilds, and restores man and his world.

If there is no one to turn to for prayers of love, a person can begin to heal himself by invoking the love concept. A young boy awakened in the night with a severe toothache. Since there were no drugs in the house to relieve the pain, he began to declare, over and over: "GOD LOVES ME. GOD IS

GUIDING ME. GOD IS SHOWING ME THE WAY." The pain subsided. He drifted back to sleep, and received permanent help from his dentist early the next morning.

Along with developing a harmonious attitude toward life through the use of love affirmations, it is also wise to speak words of love to those in your personal world, your family and friends.

An English doctor once told the Royal Society of Medicine in London, "Most people require a constant supply of appreciation for their mental health and personal happiness."

It is normal to need appreciation and kindness. Doctors have found that it is often the people who do not have enough appreciation and kindness in their lives who become physically sick or emotionally neurotic. Often words of love, appreciation, and kindness heal these people permanently, whereas the usual methods of treatment only cure them temporarily.

A lady in her eighties was placed in the hospital with numerous aches and pains. After giving her many tests, those attending her could not decide specifically what her health problem was, though they feared she was suffering from a major disease.

She remained hospitalized for weeks and received the finest of care. Yet her physical discomfort continued. Her doctors finally stated that they could not agree on a diagnosis, and her family decided to take her home. Since she lived alone, a housekeeper was employed to care for her.

The housekeeper was a Truth student who knew the healing power there is in feeling loved and appreciated. She told her patient funny stories and did many nice things for her. She often spoke words of appreciation to her, which made the patient very happy.

Within a month all the aches and pains were gone, and the previously sick, unhappy woman returned to an active, healthy life. Later, that wise housekeeper said to a friend: "TLC did it. Apparently that's what she needed—'tender, loving care.' "

Love possesses marvelous powers. A good way to test its powers is by practicing the love concept with members of your own household. Why run hither and yon, trying to find someone on whom to bestow love, when those in your own family probably need it as much as anyone? If you really want to prove the marvelous power of love, begin at home.

A well-known psychologist and marriage counselor has said that words can make or break a marriage. His advice is simple: "Always look at your marriage partner with eyes of love. Praise, don't blame. There is plenty to praise if you look for it, so look for it!"

THE FREEING POWER OF LOVE

The love concept includes freeing those we love to find their good in their own way, rather than feeling that our love for them gives us the right to possess, dominate, or criticize them.

True love frees; it does not bind. We never lose love by freeing it. Instead, through the act of release, we draw to us that love which is ours by divine right, and it becomes a stabilized, soul-satisfying form of love.

A mother once asked a friend, "How shall I prevent my daughter from marrying without my consent?"

The answer given was an interesting one: "By keeping your will in tune with the divine will. Your daughter's will is worthy of consideration, too. Your daughter, through the all-knowing Mind within her, has chosen exactly the right avenue through which her soul may have its best training in the great school of life. In the infinite scheme of things, all apparent inequalities are being adjusted through the people and events she draws to her. You must relax and let them be so, through the flow of events.

"All the challenges you meet in life are for your instruction as well as your daughter's. Your child is choosing according to an unerring law the path set forth by her subconscious history, and you have no right to any will other than the divine will in the matter.

"Perhaps you wish to save her from some experience you had? If the experience is necessary for her soul growth, you cannot prevent it, though you may postpone it. All of life is learning. If you would prevent your daughter's marrying against your will, then change your will. Affirm God's Will in the matter. Then release her to the Father, so that His Will, not yours, can become manifest."

The affirmations suggested for the mother's use were: "MY LOVE DOES NOT BIND YOU, NOR MY NEED HOLD YOU. I RELEASE YOU TO THE FATHER. I AM IN TRUE RELATIONSHIP WITH ALL PEOPLE AND ALL SITUATIONS NOW. ALL THINGS CONFORM TO THE RIGHT THING IN THIS SITUATION NOW, QUICKLY AND IN PEACE."

So often, well-meaning but possessive people have poured forth the substance of their love into the lives of other people, and have depleted themselves. The love concept frees us from trying to run other people's lives or deplete our own: "DIVINE LOVE IS NOW WORKING THROUGH ME TO ADJUST ALL THE DETAILS OF MY LIFE. LOVE TRANSFORMS MY LIFE NOW."

LOVE AND WISDOM UNITED

On an ancient Greek temple were inscribed the words, "Love tempered with wisdom is the secret of life."

Whereas mind power unaccompanied by love can

become cold and unloving, so love acting alone may become impulsive. United with wisdom, love knows the true course, so that discordant conditions of mind and body can be harmonized.

As you set about developing the love and wisdom concepts, declare often "DIVINE LOVE AND WISDOM ARE UNITED IN ME." The union of these two mind powers brings balance into your consciousness and your life.

If you have been mentally fighting anything in your life, rest your overworked mind and emotions by declaring often, "DIVINE LOVE AND WISDOM ARE UNITED IN THE SITUATION, EXPRESSING THROUGH IT PERFECTLY." Then loose it and let it go: "I BLESS EVERY SITUATION IN MY LIFE WITH LOVE AND WISDOM. LOVE AND WISDOM ARE UNITED IN ME, EXPRESSING PERFECTLY THROUGH EVERY PHASE OF MY LIFE NOW."

A prayer statement which I placed under the glass on my desk several decades ago gradually helped transform my life. It was: "I AM THE ILLUMINED CHILD OF GOD, FILLED WITH THE SPIRIT OF DIVINE LOVE AND WISDOM, BY WHICH I AM GUIDED IN ALL MY WAYS AND NOW LED INTO THAT WHICH IS FOR MY HIGHEST GOOD."

All sorts of personal difficulties simply vanish, when people daily meditate on the balancing powers of love and wisdom.

SUMMARY

1. To practice consistently the love concept is one of the quickest ways to overcome all difficulties and to demonstrate your spiritual heritage of abundance.

2. Since the word *concept* means "something conceived in the mind," the way to practice the love concept is to

become filled with the idea of love inwardly, and then express it both inwardly and outwardly.

3. Practicing the love concept releases a high-powered energy, which is instantly felt and responded to by people and situations.

4. Scientists have predicted that bombarding people and situations with thoughts of love could become a universal prescription for curing the world's ills.

5. The mind's eternal duty is to express in love. Mind power can become unbalanced when it is not used lovingly.

6. Practicing the love concept can do more to help you achieve your goals than all the hard mental effort in the world. If you get too tense about what you want out of life, you can actually repel the very good you are trying to manifest.

7. Use of the love concept magnetically draws your good to you and takes the strain out of demonstration.

8. You can begin invoking the love concept by reflecting often upon the statement: "GOD IS LOVE." This keeps you from becoming too cold and unloving. Dwelling on this statement opens the way for a marvelous transformation to take place in you and in your world.

9. The word *love* produces a positive, harmonious, magnetic current, when deliberately sent forth, which breaks up opposing thoughts of hate and renders them powerless, thus dissolving inharmony in the mind of the thinker and in the mind of everyone with whom he comes in contact.

10. Affirm often that divine love and wisdom are united in you. The union of these two mind powers brings balance into your consciousness and your life.

PROSPERITY THROUGH DIVINE RESTORATION

— Chapter 10 —

One of the least known ways of demonstrating prosperity is that of dwelling on the idea of "divine restoration."

If you could trace back in memory the cause of the unhappy experiences in your life, you would doubtless discover that most experiences of ill health, financial difficulties, and human relations problems were related to a belief in loss.

All of us have felt that at certain times in our life we lost something, and that because of that loss we have had hard experiences. You often hear people say: "My problem began when I lost my husband (or wife) . . . when I lost my health . . . when I lost my business . . . when I lost my good reputation."

Mail that comes to me from around the world reveals that the one writing usually feels his problems began because of some loss in his life. A former business executive, who now has financial and health problems, feels his troubles began when he lost his fiancée to another man many years ago. An unhappy woman feels that all her problems of ill health, financial lack, and personal unhappiness stem from the fact that she was born prematurely, fifty years ago! Her belief—that the loss of another month in her mother's womb hurt her chances for a good life—has led her from one problem to another ever since. Loss of parents or loss of love in childhood causes many a problem-ridden person to cling to those problems years later.

The thought of loss lodged in the conscious and subconscious phases of the mind causes many—perhaps most—of life's difficulties.

It's amazing how literally the thought of loss manifests itself in the little as well as the big experiences of life. I once knew a schoolteacher who was constantly losing things: items of clothing, personal effects, car and house keys, schoolbooks from which she taught, etc. She often said, "Everything has gone wrong in my life since I lost my husband."

Years previously her husband had divorced her, leaving her with small children to rear alone. This she had done successfully. But in the process, she had "lost her health." Conversation with her quickly revealed that she still suffered the thought of severe loss; that she had never forgiven her husband for leaving her with children to rear alone. This thought of loss had reflected itself as loss of health, as lack of any attempt to establish a happy life in another marriage, and as the almost daily loss of various items in her workaday world.

When she learned how to invoke the decree of divine restoration, she was gradually able to rid her mind of the belief in loss. She regained her health, moved to another part of the country, and began a new life, free from the daily agitation of losing household and personal items.

A professional woman had "lost" her husband through death. From that time on, she frequently got lost when driving her car. Road maps and instructions did not seem to help. One day she realized that she was losing her way on the highway because she still harbored the thought of loss emotionally.

As she began calling on the law of divine restoration she felt led to make a wheel of fortune (see Chapter 4) for the way of life she truly desired, rather than continuing to dwell on past losses. The act opened the way to new work in a new location, which in turn led to a happy new life for her.

Incidentally, the decree, "THERE IS NO LOSS IN SPIRIT— THE ORIGINAL ARTICLE OR ITS DIVINE EQUIVALENT NOW MANIFESTS," is a fine affirmation, which countless people have used for lost items, with good results. A merchant who had lost a family ring of great sentimental value found it two years later at his sister-in-law's house, after using this decree. A schoolboy found his lost wallet with his dollar bill in it, a year after he had lost it, on a rainy day in the mud near his school. Both he and his mother had affirmed for a year that there was no loss in Spirit, and that the wallet or its equivalent would be returned to him.

THE WORD *LOSS* MEANS DESTRUCTION

The word *loss* literally means "destruction," and the thought of loss held in the mind is certainly a destructive one. If you cling to the thought of loss, it will ruin your health, take away your prosperity, and destroy your peace of mind as well as personal happiness.

If you have problems of long standing which your prayers have not resolved, check to see if you are not holding to the destructive thought of loss. You are probably relating those problems to a time in your experience when you seemed to lose something or someone. You have probably been blaming that thing or person you feel you lost, as the cause of all your problems.

Since you have held to the thought of loss, you have also held to the problems it caused. So the thought of loss has continued to haunt you, bringing increased destruction and apparent loss into your life.

A powerful way to overcome the thought of loss and its consequences, is to remind yourself of this great truth: *There is no loss in Spirit. You cannot lose your good. When it seems you have lost your good, it is because your good has changed form! Remember that there can be no loss in any phase of nature. The elements of nature merely change their form. When your good seems to leave you—to fly out the window—let it go. That is good you have outgrown. Then watch for new good to come in the door!*

If a flower is cut from a rosebush, you do not say, "There will be no more roses." Instead, you know the bush will grow and roses will bloom again, because the roots have not been destroyed. *God gives the increase!* The word *restore* means "to make beautiful again," and through the right attitude about periods of apparent loss, you can restore or make your life beautiful again.

For this purpose, use often these prayers: "THERE IS NO LOSS IN SPIRIT. I CANNOT LOSE MY GOOD. I HAVE NOT LOST MY GOOD, THOUGH I MAY HAVE OUTGROWN CERTAIN PHASES OF IT. MY GOOD HAS SIMPLY CHANGED FORM. I NOW WELCOME MY NEW GOOD, WHICH COMES TO ME IN GOD'S WISE AND PERFECT WAYS. MY GOOD IS NOW DIVINELY RESTORED. MY LIFE IS MADE BEAUTIFUL AGAIN."

DECREE OF FULFILLMENT BLOTS OUT LOSS

You can resolve the thought of loss and its consequences by realizing that *a belief in present and future fulfillment blots out*

previous beliefs in loss. The mind easily accepts the thought of
fulfillment in the phrase *divine restoration,* since it is easy for
the mind to think of past good as being restored in some appropriate form of present fulfillment.

The prophet Joel was a master psychologist who pointed
out how fulfillment can come through the decree of divine
restoration; how one can bring into his life that which more
than compensates for what has gone out. He pointed out
this great success attitude to the people of Jerusalem seven
hundred years before Jesus Christ, at a time when they
were very discouraged. There had been a great plague of
locusts, which had caused much suffering and loss of crops,
so that the people were left without food to eat.

God spoke through Joel, and made the Hebrews this
promise of divine fulfillment: "I will restore to you the
years which the swarming locust has eaten . . . You shall
eat in plenty and be satisfied, and praise the name of the
Lord your God, who has dealt wondrously with you. And
my people shall never again be put to shame." (Joel
2:25–26)

"The years which the . . . locust has eaten" symbolize
those periods in your life that have seemed empty of good,
or even filled with trouble. They are the periods you are in-
clined to look back on with bitterness, condemnation, or
deep hurt. God promised to restore the Hebrews' good, and
He will restore yours, too, if you will change your thinking
about those difficult periods. Those periods of apparent loss
of good can be restored to you with accrued interest, when
you begin to believe they can. Write the word *gain* over all
the pages of your life!

Think back on those painful periods and say to yourself:
"That was not loss. That was actually an experience of
gain. I gained something good from that experience,
because I learned something from it. I grew through it, and
so I pronounce it growth. I pronounce it gain."

HOW TO HEAL THE UNHAPPINESS OF THE PAST

Like the people of Joel's time, you probably think you have years that the locust has eaten, for you may have had years when you had no joy in living, no happiness, no peace. You may have had years of which you are ashamed. (Most of us have!) Those are years you would like to forget or run away from. But you cannot forget them until you first restore them to their rightful place in your own thoughts and feelings. They cannot be shut out; they must be mentally and emotionally restored.

That is why they stay with you, and why you cannot forget them. They must be restored in your thinking as years of growth and learning, and therefore years of good— regardless of appearances. In one sense the past cannot be changed; but mentally and emotionally the past can be lifted up and recognized as a time when you were growing into greater understanding and wisdom—a time that opened the way for you to experience greater good.

You would not be the person you are today, you would not have the love, the understanding, the maturity, the depth, the compassion, the soul-searching desire for more of God's goodness in your life—if you had not had the past experiences you have been condemning. Out of the past you have grown, unfolded, and expanded your understanding and your world. So do not try to run away from the past. Do not condemn it. Just try to put it in its rightful place in your own thinking: Those experiences were for good, because through them you came forth into "a larger place" in your understanding. *Release all anxiety or condemnation of yourself or others about your past.* As Joseph said about his own unhappy past and those who caused it, after he had come through it to a larger place in his understanding, as well as to glorious good in his world: "You meant evil against me; but God meant it for good." (Genesis 50:20)

Just as God is in your present, so was He in your past. He was with you when you were having the experiences you now feel were wasted. He was there, helping you grow, leading you through those experiences (whether He seemed to be or not) toward fulfillment. If He was with you, bringing you into greater good, how could the past have been evil, futile, or wasted?

So let the years that the locust has eaten now be restored to you! They were the way your soul took to reach your present level of understanding as a child of God.

A PERIOD OF GAIN, NOT LOSS

According to the *Metaphysical Bible Dictionary*,[1] Joel symbolizes an attitude or feeling of dominion. Through his promise of restoration to the people of Jerusalem, Joel was trying to help them gain a feeling of dominion over their desolate circumstances. He knew that when a man feels in control of desolate circumstances, he is then able to gain the blessing from them—so that they no longer control him.

Those desolate years can be restored when you also begin to realize the great truth pointed out by Emerson in his essay *Compensation*, where he states that for everything you lose, you gain something. Remembering this, you can invoke the law of divine restoration. *Stop dwelling on apparent losses in your life, and start looking for the growth and gain that came through them. For every loss there has been a gain, so drop the loss and take the gain!*

When the thought of apparent loss seems to haunt you, instead of accepting it as loss, say to yourself: "THIS WAS

---

1. Published by Unity School of Christianity, Unity Village, MO 64065, 1931.

NOT LOSS. THIS WAS GAIN. I NOW DROP THE LOSS AND TAKE THE GAIN.''

Another way to restore the years the locusts helped themselves to is by reminding yourself that *God can give so much to the present moment that it seems even to fill the emptiness of the past.* This is a wonderful form of divine restoration.

A housewife and mother once proved this to her own satisfaction, when she received a letter from her estranged father, whom she had not seen in years. He asked to visit her and meet her husband and children. There had been much bitterness between her mother and father when she was a child, which had resulted in their divorce. Upon hearing from her father again, all the bitterness of the past welled up within her. But as she prayed for guidance, she got a feeling of peace about having him come for a visit. She decided it was perhaps by ''divine appointment'' that he desired to do so.

When her father arrived, he proved to be the best house guest she had ever had. They laughed, talked, and experienced a mutual companionship they had not previously known. Her father was especially congenial with her husband and children. It proved a soul-healing experience for all concerned. Indeed, it was as though their present happiness made up for the emptiness of the past.

Then her father went on his way, and six months later she received word that he had passed away in a distant city. How glad she was that the ''lost'' years had been restored between them in their last visit together.

BUSINESSMAN GETS BETTER JOB

Does the decree of ''divine restoration'' work in a practical way?

Yes! *Decrees of restoration and divine fulfillment are among the fastest-working prayers in the universe!* Why? Because the universe is flowing with abundant good for all mankind. In fact, the universe has no higher function than to manifest its goodness for and through man, its highest creation. When you hold to the thought of "gain," "restoration," or "fulfillment," you become a channel through which the universe is able to pour forth its abundant gain.

A businessman had been refused a number of pay raises and promotions, though employees with less seniority were being promoted and given general raises. It seemed a most unfair situation. This man had appealed to his superiors, to no avail.

It appeared that his good was lost completely in this situation. He was resentful, and felt that great injustice had been done him. Then he learned of the great success law of divine restoration. He learned that his good, which seemed to have been withheld or even lost in the past and present, could still be restored to him. He decreed that his good had not been lost but had only changed form.

It was at this point that he realized he had gone as far as he really cared to go in his present position. In fact, he had outgrown his present form of good. For several years he had been interested in another field of work but had lacked the courage to make the change toward it, since it would mean starting at the bottom of the pay scale again. Nevertheless, as he called on the law of divine restoration to bring forth his good of past and present, an offer was made him to go into the desired field of work. This time he found the courage to accept, though it meant a drastic reduction in immediate salary.

As he continued to affirm that the good of past and present which belonged to him by divine right was now appearing, it did! Within a year, this man was making several times his top pay in his previous job. Furthermore, he had greater freedom, responsibility, and opportunity for self-expression than the previous job ever could have offered. His accumulated good poured in and piled up, after he decreed and accepted it. The previously disappointing experience proved to be not loss but gain.

FORMER PRISONER RESTORED TO GOOD LIFE

A businessman committed a crime and was imprisoned for a number of years. His fellow prisoners said: "Your life is ruined because of having been in prison. You are marked for life."

Just prior to completing his prison term and returning to the outside world, this man learned of the success law of divine restoration, and he began decreeing that all the good which seemed to have been withheld during his years of imprisonment was being divinely restored to him. He decreed that he could still go forth to a good life, in spite of his prison record: "THE FORGIVING LOVE OF JESUS CHRIST HAS SET ME FREE FROM THE PAST, AND FROM THE RESULTS OF MISTAKES OF THE PAST. I FACE THE FUTURE WISE, FREE, AND UNAFRAID."

Upon being released from prison he was immediately offered work in which he was skilled. Soon he had accumulated enough money to go into business for himself. Within a year after getting "on the outside" again, he happily married. His wife cared nothing about his prison record. Today he is a happy, prosperous businessman leading a normal life, in great contrast to his life of a few years ago. This man dared to recognize and claim, in the present, all the blessings he did not know how to claim in the past. He proved that *no matter what mistakes or unfortunate experiences you have had in the past, you can still overcome them and make a comeback to a good way of life.*

This man proved another great truth too, about "locust periods" of lack and unhappiness through which most of us pass: Just as vines that are pruned bear better and fuller fruits, so all periods of hardship, problems, and challenges through which you pass can be regarded as times of pruning. Greater good than you have ever known before can come to you after your locust experiences, if you but dare to behold the good in those experiences, and learn and grow from them.

Thus, locust periods need not be periods of failure or loss. A surface defeat may contain the germ of transcendent success, so there need be no defeat—though there may be postponement. Success often comes one step beyond failure.

Since the trend of the soul is always upward and onward, locust periods can be times of gathering spiritual and mental forces together to go forward again. Sometimes when it seems you are going backward, it is because you are gathering your forces to go forward! Those seemingly "backward experiences" give you depth, insight, and understanding you might never gain from the easier paths of life.

THE ANCIENT SECRET OF RESTORATION

The ancients knew a secret about the universe that you should know, too. When you are aware of this universal truth, you can turn failure into success, disappointment into increased understanding, and loss into gain. The secret is this:

God, as a loving Father, has prepared unlimited, boundless good for each of His children, including you.

This good is eternal—ever available. It cannot be taken from you. When your good seems to have been withheld or taken, it is because your own attitudes and actions have withheld it! Not the attitudes or actions of others, but your own attitudes have caused the lack or have blocked the expression of your good. This universal good has countless ways of expressing, unless blocked by the thoughts of man.

Since this unlimited good is your divine heritage, it forever awaits your recognition and claim. When you do claim it and call it forth, the good will appear.

Furthermore, *all the good that you have not recognized or claimed in the past has not been lost. It has become dammed-up in the invisible, awaiting your recognition and claim of it. The good that seems lost from the past is still yours.* It has been accumulating in the invisible, just like money drawing interest in the bank. Your good still wants to manifest for you as present blessings of increased health, wealth, and happiness. *Your good wants you as much as you want it.*

It can still come to you. The more good you did not claim in the past, the more there is for you now. Knowing this, you can still claim every blessing in the present and future that you did not know how to claim in the past. *Whatever has been taken from you can be divinely restored!*

The first time I explained this ancient secret of restoration in a lecture, a housewife got so excited that she squealed with delight right in the midst of the lecture, and I had to stop speaking, to an amused audience, until she had calmed down. In the following months, she proved that her good from the past was not lost. So many new blessings came to her and her family that people asked: "What is her secret? What great power for good has she turned on in her life? Where is her Aladdin's lamp?"

HOW DIVINE RESTORATION IMPROVED
THEIR LIVES

A widow in recent times had had a very troubled life. She was lonely, in debt, unhappy in her work, and dissatisfied with her life in general. While she had friends praying with her for freedom from all her problems, she neutralized their prayers as she continued moaning how harshly life had treated her.

Finally she realized that her own negative words were her worst enemy. She became silent about all the hard experiences she had had in life, and began to decree "divine restoration," as she daily dwelled on the Biblical promise, "I will restore to you the years which the swarming locust has eaten." (Joel 2:25)

After she began praying the prayer of divine restoration, everything in her life changed. She received a promotion, with a pay increase. A friend of long standing whom she had once aided decided to show appreciation by giving her one thousand dollars. With this money she paid off debts and began to feel financially freer. Soon she married, after having been alone for twenty years. Truly, the years which the locusts had consumed were restored to her.

A businessman was heavily in debt and could see no way out. He had been in an accident, and it had taken a year of recuperation before he returned to his business activities. Meanwhile, others lacking his experience and knowledge had to be relied upon to run his business. Though conscientious in their desire to help, they almost bankrupted him. Because of his large indebtedness and lack of sufficient collateral, this man had been unable to obtain a loan from the usual lending agencies to ease his situation. He declared. "If I could obtain even five or six thousand dollars, it would meet the most pressing debts and keep my business solvent until I could get the business moving forward again."

Two definite attitudes prevailed which were keeping a solution from appearing. First, this man had sunk into discouragement and despair. There seemed no way out, nowhere to turn. Second, he felt a sense of great loss about the year he had been ill. He kept telling himself: "If only I had not been in that accident, this would not have happened. I would still be prosperous."

Such attitudes are normal for people in debt, but attitudes have to be changed before situations can change. It was suggested that this businessman affirm: "THERE IS A DIVINE SOLUTION TO THIS SITUATION. THE DIVINE SOLUTION IS THE SUBLIME SOLUTION. I GIVE THANKS THAT THE DIVINE SOLUTION APPEARS NOW!"

For his feeling of loss about the year away from work, these ideas were suggested: "Although it seems dismal at the moment, begin knowing that there need be no permanent loss in this experience. That which seems to have been lost during this year's illness can be 'divinely restored' to you, financially and otherwise." To help him establish and maintain this attitude, these words were typed on a card for him to carry in his wallet. Daily, when discouragement or a sense of loss began to envelop him, he was urged to read these words over and over: "I GIVE THANKS FOR DIVINE RESTORATION IN MY BUSINESS AFFAIRS. DIVINE RESTORATION IS NOW DOING ITS PERFECT WORK FOR ALL INVOLVED, AND THE PERFECT RESULTS APPEAR. I GIVE THANKS THAT EVERY FINANCIAL OBLIGATION IS NOW BEING MET IN GOD'S OWN WISE AND WONDERFUL WAY."

For a number of weeks, he daily decreed these ideas. No change seemed to be forthcoming at first, but he persisted in knowing that there was a solution. He persisted in claiming divine restoration.

Then one day the picture changed. He and his wife attended a family reunion, where his deceased brother's wife called him aside and said: "Years ago, when you first began buying into my husband's business (which later became your own), I felt that he overcharged you for the initial down payment. Now that he is gone, I no longer wish to retain the building that houses your business. I also want to see financial restitution made to you for the large initial payment.

"An appraiser tells me that the building is worth $25,000 if I sell it outright. However, I will be happy to sell it to you for $10,000." Further appraisals revealed that this man could obtain a total loan of $16,000. After purchasing the building, he still had $6,000 to clear up pressing debts and have operating cash. As these affairs unfolded, he was filled with new hope and received increased business, which helped to bring order and prosperity out of previous chaos and failure. Divine restoration did take place for him, after he began to believe that it could.

DECREE OF RESTORATION BRINGS NEW LOVE

A divorced woman proved the power of decrees of restoration for bringing new love into her life. Her husband had left her with small children. It seemed an unhappy and disappointing experience. Her family urged her to sue him for nonsupport, and they spoke of him harshly. However, she refused to condemn him and told her family she wanted to be free from all the bitter, unhappy, negative feelings that would be generated by further discussion of her unhappy marriage. She knew her husband had never found his true place in life, and that he was still confused and uncertain about many things. She also knew that what she fought to get from him, she would have to fight to keep.

Instead of negatively discussing the situation, she began affirming: "MY GOOD CANNOT BE WITHHELD FROM ME. SOMEWHERE, SOMEHOW, SOMEDAY THE GOOD THAT SEEMS

LOST IN THIS EXPERIENCE WILL BE RESTORED TO ME AND TO MY CHILDREN. OUR GOOD WILL STILL COME TO US, AT THE RIGHT TIME, IN THE RIGHT WAY, THROUGH THE RIGHT CHANNELS.''

The woman then returned to her career. Later she heard from her former husband, saying that he had joined the armed forces. He advised that he had made an allotment to their children; that they would receive monthly support payments, which they did. Later he helped to pay for their education, too.

Meanwhile, this woman worked hard in her chosen career. Just as she reached the top, she met a fine man who gave her and her children the love, the emotional security, and the understanding that seemed to have been withheld from them in the past.

Her decree had come true: The good that previously had seemed lost to her was now restored. Her good came, with accrued interest, at the right time, in the right way, through the right channels.

A businessman lost his wife to another man. It seemed a bitter loss. One day this man read: "If the beloved were still thine, none could have removed the beloved. When the half gods go, the gods arrive. 'I will restore.' "

These words helped him to release the bitterness, disappointment, blame, and criticism he had felt about his wife's desertion. It helped him to gain peace of mind and to look forward to divine restoration. In due time he happily married again. Then he literally knew what had been meant by the promise, "I will restore."

HOW TO CALL ON DIVINE RESTORATION

There is a saying "What God has given cannot be diminished." Dare to look back on those experiences in your life when it seems your good did not come forth, and boldly decree: "My good was not lost in that experience. The good can still reappear."

A man looked back on an unhappy experience of twenty years before. He had always felt that his good was destroyed by other people in that experience. After learning of the prayer of divine restoration, he began decreeing for that troublesome memory: "My good was not lost in that experience. Somehow my good will reappear."

Amazingly enough, it came through the very people who had acted badly toward him previously. They decided to do for him, in the present, what they had not done for him two decades before.

Always there is a balancing, restoring power for good at work in every person, and in every experience of loss. Your good of past and present can still appear, when you adopt a new attitude and *expect* it to appear. It may still come through the situations or people who seemed previously to have wronged you. More often, though, your good will come in an entirely new experience, which will more than compensate for the old ones. As one writer has affirmed, "Other times and other men will do me justice."

RESTORATION COMES UNDER DIVINE TIMING

Divine restoration comes in "divine timing," however— not in human timing, which wants it right now. It is an unfolding process.

That "divine timing" sometimes comes at the end of an old cycle, or it may come at the beginning of a new one. Also, there are returning cycles when we again have a chance at an opportunity that we had previously let slip from us. In my own life I have observed these returning cycles several times and have welcomed them as opportunities to compensate for previous blunders or "sins of omission."

Thus you should not be disturbed when an anticipated benefit does not become yours at some precise moment. Divine restoration is always at work, and at just the right moment it will appear in divine timing.

Instead of trying to force your good of past or present to you in the way *you* think best, open all channels by decreeing: "MY GOOD IS NOT LOST. MY GOOD NOW APPEARS IN GOD'S WISE AND PERFECT WAYS." Then let it come, through whom it will. This attitude opens the way for endless good to come to you in endless ways. Declare often for this purpose: "ALL DOORS ARE NOW OPEN. ALL CHANNELS ARE NOW FREE. THE WHOLE WIDE WORLD SAYS YES TO ME!"

You can invoke divine restoration by decreeing often: "I CALL ON THE POWER OF DIVINE RESTORATION. MY GOOD OF PAST AND PRESENT IS NOW DIVINELY RESTORED TO ME. ALL THE BLESSINGS THAT SHOULD HAVE BEEN MINE ARE STILL AVAILABLE TO ME, IN WHATEVER PRESENT FORM IS BEST. THEY HAVE NOT BEEN LOST. THEY STILL COME FORTH IN GOD'S OWN WISE AND PERFECT WAYS. I CLAIM MY PRESENT BLESSINGS TOO. THE GOOD THAT IS FOR ME NOW PRESSES UPON ME, AND I AC-CEPT IT. I AM RECEIVING NOW: I AM RECEIVING MY HIGHEST GOOD OF MIND, BODY, AND AFFAIRS NOW! MY ACCUMULATED GOOD OF PAST AND PRESENT NOW POURS FORTH INTO MY LIFE AS RICH BLESSINGS. THIS IS A TIME OF DIVINE FULFILLMENT. I WELCOME MY ACCUMULATED GOOD NOW. I GIVE THANKS FOR DIVINE RESTORATION IN MIND, BODY, AND AFFAIRS!"

SUMMARY

1. One of the least-known ways of demonstrating prosperity is by dwelling on the ideas of "divine restoration."

2. The thought of loss, lodged in the conscious and sub-conscious phases of the mind, causes many of life's difficulties.

3. The word *loss* literally means "destruction," and the thought of loss held in the mind is a destructive one. If you cling to the thought of loss, it can ruin your health, take away your prosperity, and destroy your peace of mind, as well as your personal happiness.

4. A belief in present and future fulfillment blots out previous beliefs in loss.

5. You can establish such a belief in present and future fulfillment by realizing that:

   a) There is no loss in Spirit, or in all the universe. You cannot lose your good. When it seems you have, it is because your good has changed form. The old good is good you have outgrown, so let it go.

   b) The word *restore* means "to make beautiful again." Decrees of divine restoration blot out previous beliefs in loss, and make your life beautiful again.

   c) There are returning cycles when you are again given a chance at an opportunity that you had previously let slip from you. These returning cycles come in "divine timing," when you are ready for them in your soul growth.

6. Stop dwelling on apparent losses in your life, and start looking for the growth and gain that came through them. For every loss there has been a gain, so drop the loss and take the gain!

7. As you affirm divine restoration, so much good can be added to the present that it seems even to fill the emptiness of the past. In the process, whatever has been taken from you is divinely restored.

8. No matter what mistakes or unfortunate experiences you have had in the past, you can still overcome them and make a comeback to a good life by dwelling on divine restoration.

9. When your good seems to have been withheld or taken, it is because your own attitudes and actions have withheld it—not the attitudes or actions of others.

10. There is a cosmic secret: The good that you have not recognized or claimed in the past has not been lost. It has become dammed-up in the invisible, awaiting your recognition and claim of it. The good that seems lost from the past is still yours, in whatever present form is for your highest good. When you decree divine restoration, you release that stored-up good.

11. Decrees of divine restoration can bring new prosperity, health, and love into your life, quickly and in order.

12. Always there is a balancing, restoring power for good at work in every person and every experience of loss. Instead of trying to force your good, affirm that it is now divinely restored in God's own time and way. Then your good of past and present can still appear.

In Conclusion . . .

OPEN YOUR MIND
TO RECEIVE

Your deliberate words of receiving will open the way for the other prosperity techniques described in this book to culminate as prosperous results in your life.

Why should we deliberately open our mind to receive? Because most of us have endured a pinched, narrow existence for no good reason, and we have blocked our supply in the process. There is nothing divine about a pinched existence. There is nothing spiritual about a narrow way of life. Anyone who leads a pinched, narrow existence is not expressing his divine nature.

But there is something we can do about it. The word *receive* means to accept. In order to demonstrate prosperity, we must accept it mentally first.

Psychologists tell us this: We can have anything we can

mentally accept, but we must mentally accept it *first*. A great part of the act of receiving is accepting the good we want mentally, rather than mentally resisting it.

Many people fight their good—thinking they cannot have it or that they should not be asking for it—thereby slowing down its manifestation or stopping it altogether. You may have already gotten free of such ridiculous attitudes, through your study of the prosperous truth. Such limited attitudes are not part of a child of God. As the child of a King, you have no right to limit yourself with such false ideas.

As you begin to follow through on the prosperity methods suggested in this book, open your mind and your life to receive the unlimited supply that is your divine heritage. Do so by deliberately speaking the word of receiving. Declare: "IT IS THE FATHER'S GOOD PLEASURE TO GIVE ME THE KINGDOM OF UNLIMITED SUPPLY, AND IT IS MY GOOD PLEASURE TO RECEIVE IT. I AM RECEIVING. I AM RECEIVING NOW. I AM RECEIVING ALL THE WEALTH GOD HAS FOR ME, AND GOD HAS UNLIMITED WEALTH FOR ME NOW!"

PROSPEROUS THINKING MAY BRING CHANGES

Prosperous thinking often demands changes in you and around you—changes that you are ready for and need, but tend to resist unless you know what is happening. You may seem helpless to stop these changes when they begin. Most of us have wandered away from the prosperous truth. The ideas in this book can help us get back on the right track, but we must take what goes with the use of these prosperity principles—even if it means changes involving people, places, or things.

As you open your mind to prosperity, if a rearrangement comes, you can know it is for good. You will find your life becoming happier, your prosperity and peace of mind greater.

So relax, let go, and let prosperous thinking do its perfect work in your life. Dare to open your mind to receive!